YESTERDAY'S BABIES

A History of Babycare

Diana Dick

YESTERDAY'S BABIES

A History of Babycare

THE BODLEY HEAD
LONDON

To my parents, Eric and
Mary Fairclough

British Library Cataloguing in Publication Data

Dick, Diana
Yesterday's Babies; a history of babycare
1. Infants—Care and hygiene—History
1. Title
649'122'09   RJ101

ISBN 0 370 31068 3

Printed in Great Britain for
The Bodley Head Ltd
32 Bedford Square
London
WC1B 3EL
by The Bath Press, Avon

First published 1987

Contents

List of Illustrations

1. 'Birth of the Virgin' by Israhel van Meckenem (National Gallery of Art, Washington; Rosenwald Collection)
2. 'Birth of the Virgin' by Giotto (Museo Civico di Padova)
3. An engraving showing how the lungs of an apparently lifeless baby could be inflated by means of a small tube and bellows (Wellcome Institute Library, London)
4. An incubator, or *couveuse*, at Dr Budin's Clinic, Paris (from Sadler's *Infant Feeding by Artificial Means*)
5. A medieval picture of a baby being fed by means of a horn (Wellcome Institute Library, London)
6. Illustration of a breast pump from Omnibonus Ferrarius *De Arte Medica Infantium*, 1577 (Wellcome Institute Library, London)
7. Hugh Smith's Bubby Pot (Cow & Gate Limited)
8. 'Nursing Twins' by Pieter Gerritsz van Roestraten (photograph by courtesy of Sotheby's)
9. 'Visit to the Child at Nurse' by George Morland (Dr T. G. H. Drake Collection, Museum of the History of Medicine, Academy of Medicine, Toronto)
10. Painting of a fifteen-week-old baby holding a wooden feeding bottle, 1593 (by courtesy of Sotheby's)
11. Sucking bottle made of pewter (Cow & Gate Limited)
12. An illustration (from Sadler's *Infant Feeding by Artificial Means*) showing direct suckling from asses
13. 'A City dairy in Golden Lane' by C. J. Richardson from a sketch by G. Scharf, 1835 (Greater London Record Office, Maps and Prints)
14. 'The Cobham Family' attributed to Hans Eworth (Reproduced by permission of the Marquess of Bath, Longleat House, Warminster, Wiltshire)
15. Cornelia Burch aged two months, 1581 (The Viscountess Kemsley)

34. The more stable deep-bodied pram, favoured until the 1930s (Jack Hampshire, The Baby Carriage Collection)
35. A modern baby buggy (Mothercare)
36. The Baby Walk or Gin (Antony and Peter Miall)
37. The Standing Stool (Antony and Peter Miall)
38. Child in Baby Chair (The Bodleian Library, Oxford, Douce Portfolio)
39. 'Woman making Lace' by Nicolaes Maes (The Metropolitan Museum of Art)
40. 'The Christening' by Emma Brownlow (reproduced by permission of the Governors of The Thomas Coram Foundation for Children)
41. 'The Christening Feast' by Jan Steen (reproduced by permission of the Trustees, The Wallace Collection, London)
42. 'Foundling Girls in the Chapel' by S. Anderson (reproduced by permission of the Governors of The Thomas Coram Foundation for Children)
43. Small children trying to learn their letters in a Dame School (Antony and Peter Miall)

Acknowledgements

I would like to thank Professor John Walker-Smith, Dr Rosemary Utidjian, Dr Cecil Symons, Jean Stogdon, Gabriella Gray and Alida Saunders for their help, and my husband who suggested the title. My thanks are also due to Noreen Marshall of the Bethnal Green Museum of Childhood, Jack Hampshire of the Baby Carriage Collection, Biddenden, Kent, and Colin Masters of the Thomas Coram Foundation for Children; and to the Librarian and Staff of the British Library, The Guildhall Library, The Royal College of Midwives, the British Medical Association, and especially to the Wellcome Institute Library and the Hampstead Garden Suburb Library for their unfailing help.

Introduction

'she gave birth to a son, her first born. She wrapped him in his swaddling clothes and laid him in a manger'
Luke. Chapter 2.

For many of us this is probably the earliest reference to child care that we can recall, yet what were swaddling clothes—and did the baby have to be completely re-wrapped every time he was wet? To my surprise, I found that the answer to these questions was not readily available. Yet there must have been problems. How did a family in the past set about the task of making up a feed when the mother's milk failed? If a wet nurse could not be found, did the baby starve? And although old paintings suggest that walking frames have hardly changed in design over the centuries, it seems odd that it took so long to put the cradle on wheels. Why is the perambulator essentially an invention of the Victorian age? Was there some fundamental change of thinking about babies that preceded the emergence of the pram?

I could find no book which dealt with the history of babies and toddlers. There were histories of childhood of course, but these mostly dealt with older children. By the time the child has reached three or four years of age, it can easily adapt to the environment in which it lives, so that the social history of these older children very much reflects that of their parents. But babies are unique, their demands and needs do not adapt for some time to that of the society into which they have been born. At birth, they cannot eat roast beef or, for that matter, curry, even though within a few years they will be capable of doing both.

Although I could not find any comprehensive book on the history of babies' care, there were of course many books that dealt with specific aspects, notably the history of clothes and nursery furniture, and of perambulators. While in the old medical books, especially of the eighteenth century, there is a wealth of information and guidance for the young parent. And I was surprised by the very down to earth and, in many ways, modern advice which these contained.

One book by its references led to another, and gradually a fascinating picture emerged, particularly of the seventeenth- and eighteenth-century family in this country. I was amazed to discover that there had always been a sizeable number of mothers who did not wish to breast feed—and the wet nurse system, which they created, had a major effect on the structure of family life in the past, while the Elizabethan and eighteenth-century attempts to alleviate child poverty and neglect were far ahead of their time in concept. It seemed to me that this was a subject that might well interest others, for after all we were all babies once, and already our upbringing has become a part of history!

YESTERDAY'S BABIES

A History of Babycare

1

How It All Began

Until about fifty years ago, most babies that were born in this country were delivered at home. But although this was the most likely arrangement, it was not the only possibility, even in the middle ages. In the fifteenth century, Sir Richard Whittington, the legendary Lord Mayor of London, had provided an eight bedded chamber for the use of unmarried mothers. Here, he insisted that the details of their confinement be kept secret, so as not to prejudice any chance of a subsequent marriage.[1] However, such Lying-in Charities were not only intended for unmarried women, and there were several small nursing homes, like those attached to St Mary's Without Bishopsgate and Holy Trinity in Salisbury, that offered to care for the mother during the birth and long recovery period which followed. For it was customary that the mother should be confined to bed for at least four weeks after her delivery, and this must have been difficult in households where bedrooms, and for that matter, beds, were shared. Presumably, these charitable establishments were originally intended for the poor, but in Elizabethan York, Mrs Vavasour, a local doctor's wife, would appear to have run a fee-paying clinic in her own home, where she undertook the care of several mothers and babies at one time, and even arranged for the infants to be christened, in the week following their birth.[2]

After the reformation, these institutions seem to have disappeared, but by the seventeenth century, the very poor, or those who had no one to look after them, were often delivered at the local workhouse, returning to their families when the lying-in period was over. However, the facilities available to a mother in such a place would have been no safer than those of her own home, and the risk of cross infection was much greater. Improved medical conditions, such as they were, did not come until after 1730, when the first Lying-In Hospitals were built in this country.[3] Like the workhouse, they were intended for poor women who could not afford to make any better arrangements, but a mother with any sort of social pretensions would still expect to be delivered in the comfort of her own home.

Nowadays, tests will confirm a pregnancy within a few weeks of conception, but in the past it was often months before a woman's medical advisers were prepared to make a firm diagnosis, and even then they could be wrong. Perhaps the most glaring example of a mistaken pregnancy was that of Mary Tudor.[4] Married for the first time at the age of thirty-eight to a man ten years her junior, she was convinced within a few months of her wedding that she was pregnant. Whatever their reservations about her age and general health, her physicians would appear to have gone along with the diagnosis, and when the Queen joyfully reported that she could feel the baby moving for the first time, arrangements were set in hand for her confinement.

Early in April, she moved with her whole Household to Hampton Court and prepared for her lying-in. While she waited there, three beautiful babies, no more than a few days old, were brought to see her. All three were said to have been born to a woman of low stature and great age, like the Queen, and what was more their mother was reported already fully recovered from her great ordeal. With such an encouraging example, the Queen looked forward to her own imminent delivery, but as May dragged into June, and June into July, it became increasingly apparent that the doctors had made a terrible mistake and that she had never been pregnant in the first place. In early August, the daily prayers for her safe delivery ceased abruptly, and the Court moved hurriedly on to Oaklands, making no further public statement about the birth. The poor Queen's humiliation must have been complete when her young husband left England a few weeks later, making it very clear for all to see that he could not afford to waste any further time comforting his barren wife.

Even when the confirmation of pregnancy was correct, calculations of the expected date of birth were by no means as accurate as today. This was unlikely to have been much of a problem to the poor mother, who only needed to call on a friendly neighbour for assistance when the labour started. Such women were used to helping at the confinements of friends and relatives, and one with more natural skills than the rest would have been designated to the role of midwife. In some cases, a married woman might earn a living for her family by acting as nurse to the village, but she would have had no formal training for her task.

However, the wealthy family would have made quite elaborate arrangements in advance. The nurse invariably moved into the household before the event, and in some cases, due to the uncertainty about dates, had to wait there for several months. In 1609, Maria de Medici's midwife had already been in residence for more than two months when she complained that she was losing other valuable clients as a result. The anxious King offered her 300 crowns by way of compensation for this loss of business, adding that she should have a further 200 crowns should the expected child turn out to be a boy. In the event he did not need to pay this bonus, as the Queen gave birth to a daughter. This little princess, christened Henrietta Maria, was later to play her part in history as the ill fated wife of Charles I.[5]

Although ante-natal care as we know it today did not exist before this century, it was common for mothers who could afford to do so, to take to their beds late in pregnancy in anticipation of the event. And we are told that Mary, Queen of Scots took to her lying-in chamber with great ceremony some sixteen days before her son was born. Only the woman's personal attendants and her midwife would remain with her after this, and all strangers, especially men, were excluded from the room. During the preceding months the expectant mother would have assembled the new baby's layette, as well as those things that the nurse would need for the delivery. If she had any queries she could always consult Thomas Deloney's book *The Gentle Craft* which had been published in 1597.[6] High on the list of requirements were soap and candles, as well as a low stool for the midwife to sit on. More specialised items, like the birthing chair, would be provided by the midwife, who carried such things with her from one confinement to the next.

The prospective godparents or gossips, as they were often

called, were summoned as soon as the woman showed signs of going into labour, for they needed to be available for the christening, which took place shortly after birth. Gossips, their name derived from God-Sib, literally God relative, also gave their name to the idle talk or chatter which must have occurred amongst these ladies, as they waited for the birth of their godchild. They were certainly not idle in other ways, and expected to work hard over the following two, or even three days, until the baby was safely delivered. An account of how such a labour should be conducted was given by Jacques Guillemeau in his book written in the early seventeenth century. In a volume encouragingly entitled 'The Happy Delivery of Women', he explained how a board was placed across the foot of the bed for the mother to brace herself against, and a broad band placed beneath her back. With the help of this binder, two of these ladies would pull the mother up to the sitting position with each succeeding contraction, while two more were required to hold her shoulders down. At the same time, others would take turns to hold her hands and generally keep her spirits up, as the midwife gently stroked the unborn baby downwards towards delivery.[7]

However, he advised that the mother should be encouraged to walk around for as long as possible in labour, since the pain was likely to be worse if she took to her bed too early. And it is interesting, in view of the current controversy about delivery techniques, that he should have allowed women to be delivered in a variety of ways, some in bed, others preferring a chair, or standing with support, or even kneeling—but in his opinion, the best and the safest, was in bed.

Whatever the circumstances, the actual birth, until fairly recent times, was a hazardous venture. Many young women died in childbirth, and the prayers and good wishes that survive in letters of the time recognised this awful possibility. As soon as her pregnancy was confirmed the mother was likely to receive promises of well tried amulets from anxious relations and friends, while if she was very lucky she might even be able to borrow a precious eagle stone to protect her until she was safely delivered. And the Churching service which followed the mother's recovery was no mere formality, but a heartfelt thanksgiving for what it described as the 'great pain and peril of childbirth'.

One of the greatest perils was the effect of childhood rickets on the mother's pelvis. The deformity it produced often reduced the diameter of the birth canal so that the baby's head was too large to go through. Such a delivery must have been horrific, for the poor woman would labour for days without relief. When it became clear that no progress was being made and that the outlook was desperate, the midwife would try to hook a strap or fillet under the baby's chin or around its leg, so that she could pull it down. At such a late stage in labour this manoeuvre was easier said than done, and if it failed, then both mother and baby were likely to die from the infection that this interference had unwittingly introduced. But should the baby die before this infection got a hold on the mother's bloodstream, then if it was quickly delivered, the mother might be saved against all odds. So the dead baby would be removed piecemeal, and after many hours of labour and manipulation the poor woman would have a stormy convalescence, her only doubtful consolation the fact that such an infection would probably prevent her ever getting pregnant again.

Nowadays, of course, any degree of disproportion between the baby's head and the mother's pelvis is recognised well before labour starts, and if it is clear that a normal delivery is not possible, then the child will be delivered by caesarean section. Often a disappointment emotionally, it at least guarantees a live mother and baby. But until the discovery of anaesthetics in the mid nineteenth century, it was not feasible to remove the child from the mother's abdomen in this way. Caesarean section, as this operation is now called, had been known to the ancient Egyptians, but it was only done to rescue a live baby from the womb, when the mother had died suddenly.

The possibility of a woman surviving the shock of such an operation without an anaesthetic was highly unlikely, although there were occasional claims of success over the centuries, but they were exceptional. In 1671, Mrs Sharpe wrote that she had read of such cases, but knew of none, and would not wish such a fate on any woman while she was still alive.[8] But like many others, she attributed the term Caesarean birth to the fact that Julius Caesar had been born in this manner. This would seem improbable, but he may have given his name to the law that ordered the baby's immediate removal from the womb, when a pregnant woman was struck dead by an eclamptic fit. Other authorities have argued that this term had nothing to do with the Emperor, but was derived from the Latin, *Partus Caesareus*, from *Caedere*—to cut.[9]

But whatever the origin of this term, the first caesarean section where both mother and child survived, was said to have been done by an illiterate Irish midwife in 1738.[10] If this is true, then her success was amazing since she could have had no method of replacing the blood that was lost when she cut into the womb, nor any sterile thread that was suitable to sew it up afterwards. And the only available sources of pain relief, such as alcohol or opium, would have made both mother and baby dangerously comatose, before they took effect.

But the discovery of anaesthetic drugs, in the 1840s, that could be rapidly reversed, was a great blessing for all child-bearing women. Chloroform, in particular, appeared to be ideal for women in labour, for this anaesthetic not only helped to ease the pain of a contraction when used intermittently, but would also lead to rapid unconsciousness, when it was necessary to apply forceps or proceed to caesarean section.

This operation was still only employed when all else had failed, for the early mortality rates were appalling. By 1865, of the seventy-seven mothers who had been delivered in this way, only eleven survived.[11] But over the following years the chances of success gradually improved, and this is a tribute to the skill of these early surgeons, when it is remembered that most of these operations were done as an emergency in the woman's home, with the kitchen and its well-scrubbed table acting as a makeshift operating theatre. Since that time, the introduction of blood transfusion in the 1920s and, later, antibiotics and modern methods of anaesthesia, has transformed this procedure into an acceptably safe method of delivery, when it is needed. And in more recent years epidural anaesthesia has become very popular, for it not only relieves the pain of labour, but allows the mother to be conscious for the very first moments of her baby's birth.

But this relief of pain in childbirth was hotly disputed when it was first introduced in 1847. Many theologians felt that it was against God's will to ease this traditional travail of women. After all, God's curse on Adam and Eve had prophesied such pain when they were driven out of the Garden of Eden. Fortunately, Queen

Victoria did not let these religious scruples trouble her when she found herself pregnant with her eighth child in 1853. We are told that the first mother to receive chloroform in labour had been so thrilled with its effect that she christened her baby daughter, Anaesthesia, in its honour.[12] The Queen was more prosaic, and the new Prince was baptised Leopold after her favourite uncle, but she was no less lyrical about the effects of chloroform on her labour, having endured seven earlier confinements without its help. And when she had her last child four years later she again insisted on the help of 'that blessed chloroform'. Dr John Snow, an anaesthetist from Edinburgh, had administered the liquid by dropping it onto a rolled up handkerchief, which was held close to the Monarch's face at the height of a contraction, and this method of intermittent anaesthesia became known as 'Chloroform *a la Reine*'.[13] More importantly, it quietened all those clergymen who queried a woman's right to pain relief during a normal delivery, for if the Queen felt that she should accept its help why should any of her subjects be refused?

But if a mother's luck held and, like Queen Victoria, she was fortunate enough to have a normal delivery, then once the child was safely born the ensuing procedure was fairly traditional. First, there was the umbilical cord to be cut. The seventeenth-century *Midwives' Book* advised that the navel string should be cut about four fingers' breadth from the baby, and the stump wiped with a piece of charred linen before it was covered with clean cotton or lint. Although they seem to have done things somewhat differently in France where, according to Jacques Guillemeau, it was customary to leave a longer cord for a male child so that both his tongue and private member would attain a good length in later life. In the relaxed atmosphere of the mother's bedroom after the strain of the previous days, the Gossips would call out to the midwife to be sure to give a boy child 'good measure' whereas if it was a girl – she should 'tie it short'. For no one, it seems, wanted a talkative woman!

Having been separated from its mother, the baby was rolled up in a piece of soft linen cloth called a receiver. Jane Sharpe, the author of the *Midwives' Book*, and a midwife herself of some thirty years' standing, shrewdly observed at this point that if the child had a red complexion he was healthy, but on the other hand if he appeared white and limp, he was unlikely to survive. Aristotle, centuries earlier, had noted that midwives would squeeze blood from the cord into the lifeless baby to revive it at such times, and should the infant fail to breathe, the midwife would give it artificial respiration by blowing into its mouth.[14]

The baby was then cleaned. From antiquity, this was done by rubbing salt onto its skin, a practice that seems to have been common to many cultures, for there is mention of this in both the Bible and ancient Greek texts. Although many later disagreed with this custom and thought it a cause of skin irritation, it still seems to have been popular in some parts of England as late as the eighteenth century, when Dr Buchan counselled midwives that it was preferable to wash the baby in warm water, rather than follow this older tradition of salting. On the other hand, Mrs Sharpe liked to wash the healthy baby in wine, and only favoured warm water if the child showed signs of weakness. Afterwards, she would rub the skin with acorn oil. It is interesting that both wine and salt would have had mild antiseptic properties, which might have afforded the newborn infant a measure of protection in what would otherwise have been a very unhygienic world.

After this cleaning, the baby would be wrapped in swaddling clothes. The practice of swaddling has been recorded from Roman times, and it was common in this country until the eighteenth century. This was where the midwife came into her own, for the technique of swaddling was a matter of pride. Not only was the body of the child moulded to the correct shape, but even the head was not spared. It was said that you could recognise a Parisian child by the shape of its head, for they were all moulded to a characteristic long shape in that city![15] Certainly the successive layers of binding would have kept the baby warm, although wrapped in the mummifying bands, it would have been unable to move, or even to suck its thumb. Not that this would have unduly perturbed pre-Freudian parents.

It was common practice at this point to administer a purgative to the unfortunate child, although this might be dispensed with if the mother intended to feed her own infant, as the first milk was thought to be a natural purgative. On the other hand, if the baby was to be suckled by a wet nurse who had delivered some months earlier, then a purgative was mandatory, as her milk was regarded as 'stale'. This molesting over, the swaddled baby should be laid in a cradle and allowed to recover from the ordeal of its birth. The room was darkened for the first few days because bright light was thought to be bad for the newborn baby's eyes, and a likely cause of a later squint.

It was thought to be equally important that the mother should rest quietly without disturbance for at least the first few days after the birth to avoid any physical or emotional stress that might trigger off an eclamptic fit. This was always difficult for Royal mothers, as protocol demanded that as many officials as possible were in attendance at the time of the delivery. And if all hopes were pinned on the birth of a son—as in the case of James II's wife, Mary of Modena—then the emotion of telling her that she had at last borne an heir to the throne after fifteen years of marriage was likely to cause a brainstorm. James wisely arranged for the midwife to give him a secret signal if the child was a boy, so that the Queen could be protected from this momentous news and the courtiers' excitement, until she felt a little stronger. Even in the best of circumstances, the medical attendants usually found it politic to leave it to their Sovereign to break the news to his wife, for if anything should go wrong after that, he would have only himself to blame. Marie Antoinette was so aware of the silence after her second child had been born that she thought that she had given birth to a second daughter, and assured her ladies that she was taking the disappointment very calmly. It was Louis, with tears in his eyes, who tactfully broke the good news, with the formal request that 'Monsieur le Dauphin begs leave to enter'.

But the mother was not out of danger after the first few days, and childbirth fever was a very real threat for several more weeks. It was for this reason that her windows were sealed and the room kept very warm, for the fever was always heralded by violent shivering attacks, and it was assumed that in such cases the mother must have caught cold. However, providing she made good progress, she would be allowed to sit up after a week or so, and this milestone in her recovery was often marked by a party. So when James IV's mistress gave birth to a child, this stage in her confinement was celebrated by what was called 'the lady's upsitting feast' and four dozen rolls of white bread were specially ordered for the occasion.[16] Forty days after the birth, if all was well, the mother would leave her house for the first time to go to church for her purification, and to give thanks for her safe delivery.

But whatever the social position of the family, it was recognised that country women did best in childbirth, and when John Graunt studied the Bills of Mortality in 1662, he concluded that life for all was healthier in the countryside than in London. Yet as doctors pointed out a century later, many mothers perversely tried to come to the city for their confinement, when they would have been better advised to stay in the healthier surroundings of the countryside. Perhaps part of the attraction of a town delivery was the possibility of being attended by a new phenomenon—the male midwife.

Until the emergence of male midwives in the seventeenth century, only women were allowed to assist the mother in child-birth, and they also had to be mothers themselves. Many of these ladies were the widows of artisans, and although experienced, were seriously hampered by this lack of formal training. For they had no access to the new sciences of anatomy and physiology, since such studies, even when confined to their own sex, were generally considered to be unseemly for women.

Louise Bourgeois, a French midwife, was one of the exceptions, and perhaps because her husband was a doctor, and a friend of Ambrose Paré, she had a unique opportunity for study.[17] Her training went on for five years, a very long time in an age when midwives would normally have had no more than a few weeks' instruction from an older colleague. It certainly paid dividends, for she was entrusted, ahead of her older respected rivals, with the task of delivering Maria de Medici's first child. This poor Queen was delivered in a large pavilion, separated by no more than a thin curtain from all the nobility who had managed to crowd inside the room.[18] Whatever the expectant mother's feelings, the strain on her midwife must have been enormous.

So when, twenty-eight years later, the Queen's own daughter, Henrietta Maria was expecting a baby, arrangements were made for another experienced nurse, Madame Peronne, to be sent to England to deliver her. Unfortunately, Henrietta Maria went into premature labour at Greenwich ten weeks before her time, and Madame Peronne was still in France. The local midwife did not have Louise Bourgeois' courage and resilience, and on realising that she was expected to deliver the heir to the throne, promptly fainted! Fortunately, Peter Chamberlen was available to come to the rescue, and this male midwife safely delivered the Queen, although sadly the premature baby was stillborn.[19]

The Chamberlen family were Huguenot refugees. They had built up a reputation as successful *accoucheurs*, in spite of the traditional prejudice towards men in this role, for they were known to achieve success in cases where the female midwife had given up all hope of a happy outcome. This was largely due to the invention of the obstetric forceps, which was a closely guarded family secret, and not one that they felt under any moral obligation to share with the rest of the world. Indeed, they went to great lengths to protect their secret, covering the blades with soft clothes so that no clanking of metal would be heard, and only applying the forceps when shielded from public gaze by draperies.

Naturally, it was not long before the well-to-do London family followed this Royal example, and favoured the male midwife, even when a difficult birth was not anticipated. However, for the poor who could not afford one, and those who lived in the country, who might not find one, the female midwife was as popular as ever. On the Continent her status was higher, and such a lady was Charlotte von Siebold.[20] In 1819, she came to England to the household of the Duke of Kent, to deliver his infant daughter Princess Victoria; she then returned to Germany, where several months later she was to assist at the birth of Prince Albert.

However, by the late nineteenth century the very word midwife was considered indelicate. Indelicate or not, they were often very close to the problems of poor families. For in evidence to a Select Committee at this time, it was stated that midwives often helped babies to die when they knew that the family could not afford to feed another child. And this 'churchyard luck' as it was euphemistically called, was a recommendation to some mothers when it came to choosing a nurse.[21]

Of course, the cheapest food for the young baby was the mother's own milk, and there was no doubt in anyone's mind from the earliest times, that this was also the best nourishment for the child. Today, if a mother decides against breast feeding for her baby, she can give it a formulated milk powder, confident that it will thrive on this food. But before the present century, all attempts to find a substitute for human milk were disastrous, and contributed to the high infant mortality rate. However, in the past, mothers had a third choice, they could employ a wet nurse. Wealthy families were most likely to choose this alternative, although there were many reasons for deciding to do so, and if the mother had died in childbirth, it was imperative to find a wet nurse within the first day or so of birth. Sometimes a mother was found who had just lost her own baby, but in many cases poor women would become professional wet nurses, feeding several small babies in succession. Although Oribasus had advised that the ideal woman was between twenty-five and thirty-five years of age, and recently delivered of a male child, on many occasions it must have been a question of Hobson's choice. Wet nursing went on well into the nineteenth century, even Sir Winston Churchill had a wet nurse, and Mrs Beeton's *Book of Household Management* devoted several pages to the choosing of a suitable lady.

So, the baby having been born, bathed, swaddled and fed, was then laid in its cradle and rocked until it fell asleep. Sometimes this rocking was so violent that the tightly swaddled package fell right out of the cradle onto the floor. Such accidents must have been quite common, and the careful nurse always made sure that the child was well and truly strapped into its crib, before she started to rock it. By the late eighteenth century, the traditional cradle resting on wooden rockers was out of favour for this reason. Dr Hugh Smith preferred a cot that stood firmly on all four legs. But the idea of rocking was too good to disappear completely and some cradles for young babies were designed to be swung from a central frame, so that they could be gently pushed to and fro. Sheraton even added a clock mechanism, that once started would keep the cot going, like a pendulum, for twenty minutes or more without further help. But when the baby grew older and began to stand up it could easily topple out of such a contraption, and so the crib with high sides found favour. And the invention of the drop-side cot in the late nineteenth century meant that these cot sides could be as tall as the standing child, yet by dropping one side down the mother or nurse could easily attend to his needs.

But if, in spite of rocking and lullabies, the baby showed no signs of settling and continued to cry, it was likely to be given a small dose of opium. Country women were experts at making up this cordial, and Dr Buchan was not the only physician to comment on the large amounts that were given for this purpose, a practice that on occasion led to the infant's death. As he pointed out, a harassed nurse would always prefer to have an undemanding sleepy baby in the cradle, and some sly wet nurses would even smear a little of this drug around their nipples, for the baby to suck. Clearly, the stress that a wakeful baby can have on the family is not new, and parents then, as now, were often desperate to find a solution to the problem.

The common practice of taking the baby into the parent's bed to pacify it, was also unacceptable to medical men, and nurses too were condemned if they shared their bed with their young charges. Yet until two hundred years ago the sharing of beds was common to every stratum of society. Nevertheless, in the ninth century the Church went so far as to condemn this habit as a grievous sin, and later even insisted that the child should remain in its cradle until it was three years old.[22] The stringency of this ruling seems strange to modern eyes, but many babies were thought to have been accidentally smothered by a sleeping adult, and of course, the swaddled baby would have been powerless to move under such circumstances. 'Overlaid and starved at nurse' was given as the cause of 529 deaths in the London Bills of Mortality in the twenty years following 1639, and Dr Buchan was still warning of the dangers of such accidents in 1803. Modern evidence suggests that the danger of suffocation has little foundation in fact, unless the baby is unable to move for some reason.[23] And such shared sleeping arrangements may appeal to the breast feeding mother who can suckle her baby whenever he cries, without any further disturbance to her night's rest.

But for parents who find it difficult to get to sleep, worried by the snuffles and small noises of their sleeping baby during the night, the opposite also holds true. The experts advise that the baby should be put to sleep in another room so that only the persistent demand for food should disturb their night's peace. For in the early weeks after their baby is born, it is the parents, and not their child, that are likely to suffer from sleep deprivation! And in this early period the problems of caring for their long awaited baby can seem overwhelming. So, as with most modern advice on childcare, the final decision rests with what is easiest in the long run for the parents. There are no hard and fast rules these days, and most decisions are a matter of fine judgement. No wonder Dr Buchan concluded that all parents should be paid a premium at the end of one year's successful childrearing![24]

2

Breast is Best

When Benjamin Brand, a puritan, died in 1636, the inscription on his tombstone recorded that his wife had borne him twelve children, and that all twelve had been nourished with her own 'unborrowed milk'.[1] Although this was clearly intended to commend his spouse's maternal devotion, it was also a dig at those women who shirked their responsibilities in the matter of breast feeding. Such a rebuke was not unusual, since Puritans had always regarded breast feeding as one of a mother's most sacred duties. Nor was anyone in doubt about the value of a mother's milk to her baby, and midwives and medical men had always been anxious to encourage a mother to breast feed. Indeed, Jacques Guillemeau maintained that if a woman refused to do so, she was guilty of a crime similar to abortion, since her refusal might well imperil her baby's life.[2] So it comes as rather a surprise to find that in spite of all this urging from doctors and parsons alike, that a considerable number of women still refused to breast feed, and preferred to employ another mother to suckle their baby instead.

Whether a mother was morally bound to breast feed her own child, had always been a source of heated argument. On the one hand there were those mothers who found the idea of suckling their own baby both natural and appealing, but equally there was always a considerable number of women who found the prospect unpleasant, and even offensive. Such mothers resorted to wet nurses if they could afford them, and the large number of such nurses that were employed over the centuries gives some indication of the extent of this refusal.

Galen believed breast milk to be 'white blood' and his explanation of its origin was accepted without question by succeeding generations of doctors. He taught that, since the periods ceased abruptly with the beginning of pregnancy, they were diverted to feed the growing foetus. After the baby's delivery, this blood was driven from the mother's womb to her breasts, where it underwent a series of mysterious changes during which it lost its colour. This whitened blood was nevertheless immediately recognised as familiar food by the newborn infant, who though weak in many ways, was able to suck vigorously from birth.

So, according to Galen, this milk would continue the growth of the infant which had begun in the womb nine months before. And just as the mother had endowed her child at conception with something of her own personality, so she would continue to influence its later development through her milk. If another woman took over the task of nourishing the baby, then it would be this stranger's milk and character that would be incorporated into the complex make-up of the growing infant. There were endless discussions about the extent of this influence, very similar in many ways to the arguments about surrogate motherhood today. In general, the Church accepted the idea of wet nursing as a necessary evil, but the more censorious puritan sects were vehement in their condemnation of any woman who relinquished her maternal duty without good reason. And medical writers could point to many examples in nature to show just how drastic the effect of another woman's milk could be. For, as Thomas Phaire declared in the sixteenth century, it was well recognised that lambs that were fed with goat's milk, had 'course wolle' while kids that were fed with sheep's milk, grew up to have soft fur.[3] Such fears no doubt accounted for the frequently told story of the virtuous Queen of France, who, on discovering that a serving lady had pacified her royal baby with her less than regal milk, promptly wrapped the poor infant in a blanket, and rolled and shook him, until every drop came up. This done, the good Queen re-fed him herself. But in spite of this prompt action, the young baby never achieved the same success in adult life as his older brothers.

Certainly, doctors were only too anxious to give all the advice they could to help a mother increase her milk supply, and Thomas Phaire gave a number of well tried recipes to his readers, including one which contained, amongst its essential ingredients, the powder of earthworms! When these medicines failed, a breast pump could be tried, and Omnibonus Ferrarius showed a design for such a pump, which could be operated by the mother sucking on one end.[4] Although cynical observers commented that this lack of milk seemed, like gout, to be a disease of the rich, since the problem was unknown to the poor mother,[5] Mrs Sharpe gave it as her opinion that there were few women who could not suckle their babies, and she added that some had enough milk to feed a friend's child as well![6] Something of this kind seems to have been done by Elizabeth Fry in 1823, when she wrote that she attended the lying-in of her cousin's wife, who died nine days after her delivery. Mrs Fry recalled, 'I, suckling the babe at times, helped to support it.'[7] Since she was the mother of eleven children herself, she clearly took such charitable acts in her stride.

Those recalcitrant mothers who refused to breast feed were left in no doubt about its value, by the medical profession. The three great writers of family medicine in the eighteenth century, Hugh Smith, William Buchan and William Cadogan, did their uttermost to argue its importance. Hugh Smith, like Mrs Sharpe, refused to accept that any woman who was capable of bearing a child would be unable to feed it. And referring to the high infant mortality of his time, he pointed out that more human young died in infancy than young animals, and concluded that the denial of breast milk was the cause, since the human mother was alone in nature, in her ability to refuse her progeny this sustenance.[8]

Following a similar line of argument, William Buchan drew attention to the unnatural behaviour of those mothers who, having nourished their infant in the womb unseen, for nine months, nevertheless refused it further food after birth. He advised would-be fathers to think hard about their wives' refusal to breast feed, for if they were selfish mothers, it was hardly likely that they would make better wives.[9] Perhaps to counter the frequent objection that a mother would have no time to herself if she decided to breast feed, both Hugh Smith and William Buchan were adamant that she should only feed her baby every four hours. They were against night feeds altogether, on the grounds that both the mother and baby needed a period of enforced rest. Whether their suggestions were taken seriously by mothers, who were used to feeding their babies whenever they cried, is difficult to know.

Certainly, discussions as to whether or not to feed 'on demand' swung backwards and forwards in the following centuries. By the 1920s, medical opinion again favoured rigid feeding schedules, and any mother who dared to feed her baby at night, was dismissed as 'weak willed' by the *Mothercraft Manual*, the Dr Spock of its day.

This book, and the Mothercraft Society which was responsible for its publication, were the inspiration of a New Zealand doctor, Sir Frederick Truby King.[10] For many years he had worked as the enlightened Medical Superintendent of a lunatic asylum in Dunedin. In 1904, he visited Japan and was immediately struck by the absence of infantile gastro-enteritis which killed so many young babies in New Zealand at that time. He attributed this good health to the popularity of breast feeding in Japan, and returned to his native country to promote its value amongst parents and doctors with an almost missionary zeal. At the same time he was impressed by the arguments of many eminent European doctors that overfeeding was in part responsible for bowel upsets in young babies, and he advised that infants should only be fed for short periods, and at fixed intervals, however hard they might cry in the meantime.

At a practical level, at his weekend cottage at Karitane he and his wife cared for thirteen of the worst cases of unwanted babies that they could find, and by care and good nursing demonstrated that they could all grow into healthy children. And he countered the growing practice of bottle feeding in New Zealand at that time, with slogans such as 'Breast Fed is Best Fed'! Within five years this campaign had had the remarkable effect of halving the infant mortality rate.

At that time the infant mortality rate in England was four times that of New Zealand. So with such success behind him, his visit to Europe in 1917 made a great impression, and his magnetic personality attracted many loyal adherents to his cause. He never ceased to emphasise the value of breast milk to young babies, but if breast feeding was not possible for some reason then he advocated his own formula which was sold by the Mothercraft Society in this country. Many of his radical ideas on childcare would be undisputed today. There was a great emphasis on fresh air and light clothing for young children, but he was rigid in his adherence to the dangers of overfeeding. Sadly, it is this aspect of his teaching for which he is often remembered, and condemned, today. On his last visit to England in 1928, he had become a senile and rambling old man, insisting against all the evidence that overfeeding was the root cause of gastro-enteritis.

By this time, many mothers had suffered endless miseries with engorged breasts while their babies screamed with hunger, terrified that if they dared to feed before the appointed time they risked a serious bowel upset. It was a system that was doomed to failure in all but the most expert of hands, and paradoxically, may even have encouraged more bottle feeding since such rigid schedules are easier to observe when the baby is bottle fed. Eventually, wiser counsels prevailed and the joys of demand feeding were once more promoted. Nowadays, mothers are encouraged to feed their babies whenever they cry, and the irregular demands for food of the newborn baby soon settles down to an acceptable pattern for the harassed mother.

But whether the current fashion was demand feeding or rigid schedules, over the centuries some mothers would still resist all persuasion to suckle their own infants. As early as the fourteenth century there were complaints from some churchmen that this maternal duty was no longer in fashion. Such mothers, so it was said, did not care to feed their own babies because it ruined their figures and prevented them from 'frolicking' with their husbands.[11] Whatever the effect of breast feeding on their figures, it was certainly true that women would be advised to avoid intercourse while they were lactating. Galen had taught that seminal fluid sours the milk, and his word was law to the medieval physician. However, by the seventeenth century, Francois Mauriceau, like others, was prepared to dispute the truth of this statement, for he observed that country women, who knew nothing of Galen, or his theories for that matter, nevertheless reared beautiful children 'notwithstanding they lay every night with their husbands'. Even so, it was advisable that the mother should lead a celibate life, for although her natural fertility was reduced during lactation, there was always a danger that she might become pregnant. Should she do so, she would be obliged to stop breast feeding immediately, to conserve her strength for the unborn baby, and this sudden withdrawal of milk might have serious effects on the health of her older child.

Even if she continued to breast feed, her milk would be of poor quality, since much of its goodness was diverted to the child in her womb. For this reason, families often made it a 'condition of employment' when they hired a wet nurse, that she should live apart from her husband. Not that they seem to have had much success in enforcing this rule, for the commonest reason for changing a nurse was her unexpected pregnancy. However, before the condition was diagnosed, her young charge might have gone hungry for several months on this half-strength milk, so it is perhaps not suprising that Louis XIV's wet nurse was instantly dismissed for daring to even talk to her husband.[12]

Some mothers excused their refusal to breast feed by claiming that it was their husbands who objected to a crying baby in the bedroom at night. This may have been true on occasions, but Rousseau took a more cynical view, and reckoned that women who did not want to feed their baby for personal reasons, often inveigled their husbands into giving such excuses, or persuaded their doctor to say that they were not up to the exhausting routine of feeds. These, in his opinion, were no more than subterfuges to cover up their own selfish refusal to suckle their babies.

Of course, for the poor mother, there was no question of choice, for if she refused, her child would starve. So, finding a wet nurse for the infant was generally a privilege reserved for the noble and wealthy. A poor family would not be able to afford such luxuries, and only in the case of serious illness would the baby be fed by another. Mrs Sharpe observed that it was customary for the rich to put their children out to nurse, even though it was thought to change the natural disposition of the child. However, with the increasing affluence of the middle classes, it seems that as time went on, more and more families availed themselves of the services of a wet nurse. Sir Walter Raleigh regretted this trend, that 'taught all women but the beggar to find out nurses, which necessity only ought to command.'[13] And later in the same century, Coustel commented in the same vein that 'formerly, it was a universal custom practised by all mothers to nurse their babies themselves, but the delicacy of those who have a little bit of wealth has now become so great, that this good custom has almost entirely been abolished.'[14]

The criticisms of the fourteenth-century churchman quoted earlier show that Coustel was mistaken in believing in an earlier 'Golden Age', when all women breast fed their children. For wet nurses had existed since Roman times and beyond. But his comments do bear out a change in social behaviour, which by the seventeenth century allowed the middle classes to ape their betters in such practices as wet nursing.

Yet, at the same time, there seems to have been a number of mothers in every age, who felt equally strongly that it was important to suckle their own children, and who, in spite of the opportunity to do so, refused to employ a wet nurse. Defoe tells us that James I's Queen, Anne of Denmark, had no doubts about the importance of feeding her own children, and asked, 'Will I let my child, the child of a King, suck the milk of a subject and mingle the Royal blood with the blood of a servant?'[15] Of course, the Church had always praised the mother who decided to feed her own baby, and had been at pains to point out that no woman was demeaned by agreeing to do so. Indeed, such a sacrifice on her part only increased her female virtues, and clergymen were fond of reminding their flock that Sarah was not too proud to suckle Isaac.

By 1622, a remarkable book written by the Countess of Lincoln may also have influenced many educated mothers to breast feed. The Countess had borne no less than eighteen children herself, all of whom had been put out to nurse. However, she was moved to write a dissertation in later years on the value of maternal breast feeding, prompted by the fact that only one of her sons had survived to manhood. Her book was an attack on the wet nurse system, and powerful propaganda for mother's milk. She asked her readers to enquire of any modest loving mother if it really involved a great deal of trouble to breast feed her own infant. And referring to the frequent excuse of leaking milk spoiling their clothes and making them smell, she went on, 'Behold most nursing mothers, and they be as clean and sweet in their clothes— as those that suckle not.'[16]

Such influences seem to have gathered momentum by the eighteenth century, for a visitor to England at that time was surprised to find that 'even women of quality nursed their own children'.[17] Michael Underwood's comments confirm this trend, and he noted that it was increasingly fashionable for 'ladies of rank' to be maternally minded, so that the evils of wet nursing and baby farms were declining.[18] One such lady of rank was Georgiana, Duchess of Devonshire. In 1783, she not only suckled her baby daughter, but kept her in bed with her when she discovered the rocker, who had been employed to care for the child, was drunk. Nor did the inconvenience of feeding routines prevent Betsy Freemantle from going to a ball. But since she was 'at nurse' she decided against joining in the dancing, not that it stopped her staying out until dawn all the same. The strain of this life does seem to have caught up with her eventually though, for one month later, she wrote in her diary that the baby had been weaned![19]

This late eighteenth-century interest in breast feeding was also stimulated by the writings of Jean Jacques Rousseau. In his book *Emile*, first published in 1762, he gave an account of how he would bring up an imaginary child, and made it clear that the mother's milk was the ideal food for the young baby. No mother, worthy of the name, should lightly hand over to a hired nurse this unique opportunity to influence her child's development. It was not long before intellectual females, on either side of the channel, were persuaded to nurse 'à la Jean Jacques'. Rather suprisingly, all of Rousseau's own children were consigned to a Foundling Hospital. Nevertheless, his influence was widespread, and Dr Buchan, like other members of his profession, regarded him with great respect and approval.

Certainly, by the eighteenth century, discussion and argument as to the value of breast feeding was common, and most doctors used the appalling infant mortality rates of children who were put out to nurse to back up their advice. Dr Hugh Smith's *Letters to Married Women on the Nursing and Management of Children*, which was largely concerned with the importance of mothers' breast feeding their own babies, went into many editions, and was addressed directly to parents. The increasing number of books that were available to guide young parents on their children's upbringing reflected the growing interest in the subject, and when Princess Victoria was born, her mother, the Duchess of Kent, was determined that she should receive maternal nourishment, while her father mused on what he described as, 'an office most interesting in its nature'.[20]

Yet, in spite of this re-awakened interest in the value of

maternal feeding, wet nursing was as popular as ever, for a considerable number of mothers still refused to suckle their own children. The employment of wet nurses only fell when artificial methods of feeding infants improved sufficiently to become a safer alternative. Some writers have suggested that this refusal by mothers to breast feed is a phenomenon of the last eighty years or so, and blamed the success of bottle feeding for its decline. In reality, the arrival of safer methods of artificial feeding have ensured the welfare of those babies who might well have perished under a wet nurse regime. Today, if a mother in this country does not wish to breast feed, she can be assured that her decision is unlikely to affect her child's survival. But in the past, mothers were prepared to refuse, knowing that in so doing, they were putting their baby's life in jeopardy, yet an amazing number did make this decision, in spite of very strong medical and moral advice to the contrary.

It is interesting that the reasons put forward in the past for refusing to breast feed are very similar to those that are given today. Perhaps the most important factor in the mother's decision, as Dr Buchan recognised, is the influence and example of her own family. If a mother has been breast fed herself, then she is more likely to want to suckle her own baby. Although even then, some, like Queen Victoria, in spite of her own mother's example and Albert's encouragement, would still refuse to do so.

The Queen found the whole idea so distasteful that she tried, in turn, to dissuade her daughters from doing so. And when Princess Alice, against all her mother's advice, decided to breast feed her own child rather than expose her to the perils of infantile diarrhoea, she felt compelled to write a letter of explanation to her mother.[21] The defensive tone of this letter suggests the strength of Victoria's feelings in the matter. Yet the Queen also expressed strong opinions on the subject of frequent pregnancy, and in her later years begged her daughters to space their children, saying that the arrival of the Prince of Wales, only eleven months after the birth of her first child, was bad for her son and herself. She bitterly resented this pregnancy coming, as it did, so soon after the first. Although she recovered her good spirits after the delivery, she made no secret of her dismay each time she found herself, to use her own words, 'for it' again![22] Had she managed to overcome her feelings of repugnance, and decided to breast feed the Princess Royal, she would no doubt have appreciated the natural infertility which lactation conferred on her. And it is interesting to speculate that, had she done so, her subsequent relationship with her eldest son might well have been a much happier one.

3

Borrowed Milk

Wet nursing was a curious business. It had been recognised since the earliest times that a newborn infant would readily accept the milk of another mother, and this substitution was, quite literally, life-saving if the mother had died in childbirth or was too ill to feed her own baby. But such reasons for employing a wet nurse were relatively uncommon, and the majority of families who hired another woman to feed their baby did so in spite of the fact that the child's own mother was more than able to do so for herself. Most wealthy parents took it for granted that they would hire a wet nurse to feed their baby, and to do so was regarded as a sign of good breeding and class. As a consequence, wet nursing was a major source of employment for poor mothers, even in medieval times. Indeed, the very title of Nurse, as an English Franciscan pointed out in the thirteenth century, was derived from the word 'nourish', and it was the nurse's role to nourish the young baby.[1] But although the baby would thrive physically on this alien milk, there were other aspects of wet nursing that led many to condemn it. In spite of these criticisms however, wet nursing went on well into the second half of the nineteenth century in this country, and it was only the introduction of safer methods of bottle feeding that led to its final demise. It seems extraordinary that so little remains today of this once flourishing aspect of childcare, that as late as 1907 in France, sent nearly 80,000 babies from their homes to wet nurses in the country.[2]

To many poor women, wet nursing was a relatively easy way of bringing some much needed extra money into the home, and they would endeavour to feed a succession of such foster children for as long as possible. In theory anyway, there was no time limit to this period of suckling, although the milk of a recently delivered mother was always thought to be 'fresher' and therefore preferred to that of a woman who might have delivered a year or so earlier. If parents found themselves obliged to hire a nurse with an older baby, then it was important to enquire if her periods had re-established themselves, for if they had, her milk would be thin and lacking in nourishment.

That this cottage industry was a thriving business, even in Roman times, is borne out by Galen's comments and such wet nurses commonly plied for hire by the Colonna Lactaria.[3] Julius Caesar is said to have upbraided those Roman matrons who liked to carry a pet dog or monkey in their arms, rather than their own children whom they delegated to the care of a wet nurse.[4] Nor were such arrangements made on a casual basis, for the costs of these transactions were scrupulously entered into the household account books of the middle ages, and in fifteenth-century Florence, a merchant even entrusted the task of finding a suitable nurse to an agent. The agent's wife found a mother who had delivered only two months earlier, and reported that the woman's child, a girl, was on the brink of death. Should the baby die that night, the mother had promised to come to the merchant's house immediately after the burial.[5] But it is clear from these comments that suitable nurses must have been in short supply, as in better circumstances he would have selected a woman with a plump healthy baby, to prove the quality of her milk.

All writers emphasised the need for the nurse to be both physically healthy and of virtuous disposition, since her milk would continue the growth and development of the child, that had begun in its mother's womb. Through her milk, she would transmit her own personality, and to some extent she would become part of the baby in just the same way as its natural parents. Some even claimed that this later nurture would have more influence on the child's development than the characteristics inherited from its forebears, and Thomas Muffet was in no doubt that even the finest child would degenerate morally if fed the milk of a common servant.[6] It was beliefs like these that lay behind all the custom and concern that surrounded the practice of wet nursing. The extent of this influence was made the subject of debate in 1605, when James I visited Oxford with his Queen.[7] Although his own Court Physician, Sir William Paddie, actually spoke against the motion, the fact that it was discussed at all, in these auspicious circumstances, is an indication that it was of serious consequence to this seventeenth-century monarch and his court.

The belief that a nurse's milk could change a child, was still held in the nineteenth century and Margot Asquith recalled that her sister Charlotte was thought to be taller than the rest of the family because she had an exceptionally tall wet nurse.[8] Sometimes this effect would be of value to the baby in later life, and Michelangelo attributed his talent as sculptor to these early influences. He had been put out to nurse to a stone cutter's wife, and claimed in later life that 'with my mother's milk, I sucked in the hammers and chisels that I use for my statues.'[9] And maybe it was for this reason that, until the time of Charles I, the Prince of Wales traditionally had a Welsh wet nurse![10]

Not only was the nurse's milk thought capable of changing the child, but in its turn, whatever she ate would alter her milk, and so items of food that were thought to be indigestible to the baby were banned from her diet. For this reason she was expected to avoid all spicy dishes, and only eat meals which had been boiled or steamed. Mrs Beeton, in particular, was most anxious to warn unwary mothers of the sly nurse who secretly indulged in such indigestible foods as cucumber and fried meat. The nurse would have no after effects, but the baby would undoubtedly have an agonising colic as a result.

In the same way, it had been known since the time of Celsus that any medicines that were given to the nurse would also appear in her milk, and mediaeval physicians made good use of this route when it came to treating the young baby. The nurse would be given the draught, often containing opium in some form, and she in turn would secrete it in her milk to be suckled by the infant. The great advantage of this method was, of course, that it was most unlikely that the baby would receive an overdose, and it would be protected from the more noxious ingredients of the medieval pharmacy. Needless to say, no one was the slightest bit concerned about the effects of repeated doses of opium on the hired wet nurse.

Fear of the transmission of more spiritual food seems to have been the reason why medieval Jews compelled Christian nurses in their employ to 'spill their milk' for three days after the Easter communion, and in 1235, Henry III actually forbade such nurses from serving Jewish families, presumably for similar motives.[11] There must have been a considerable number of Christian mothers working for Jewish families, to occasion such legislation, and it is strange that more Jewish wet nurses were not available. Whatever the reason for this shortage, the fact that orthodox Jewish parents were prepared to jeopardise their infants' spiritual welfare in this way, is remarkable, and that they did so, suggests the strength of some mothers' intrinsic objection to breast feeding, even in the middle ages.

To prevent the baby from being changed by the nurse's milk, it was advisable to find a woman who resembled the child's mother in every way, and ideally she should be as well born as the child's own parents. In practice this was rare, but there was no lack of advice about the ideal woman, although there seems to have been some disagreement about the sex of the wet nurse's natural child. Some held that she would always have better milk if she had borne a son, while others, like Mrs Sharpe, thought it wiser to engage the mother of a daughter to feed a girl baby. Certainly, it was said that the wrong type of breast milk might masculinise a female, or make a boy effeminate. But all agreed that the nurse should be of mature years, although it is disconcerting to discover that William Cadogan defined middle age, in this context, as lying between twenty and thirty years! Middle-aged or not, she would probably have had several children of her own by this time, and would be experienced in handling small babies.

According to Jacques Guillemeau,[12] the wet nurse should have a pleasing countenance, clear bright eyes, well-formed nose, red mouth and very white teeth. This interest in her dental hygiene was no doubt due to the nurse's practice of chewing tough food and rolling it into little balls, before feeding it to her charge. Her neck should be strong, with breasts that were easily sucked by the young baby. He strongly disapproved of redheads, and it is interesting that in Italy, where wet nursing was still practised in the early years of this century, just these same qualities were demanded of the ideal woman—even to the extent of damning the red-haired nurse, because her milk would have an unpleasant smell, three centuries after Guillemeau had made the same observation. Much the same sentiments were expressed by a Victorian writer, who also demanded that the woman should be free from any vulgarity, as well as being imbued with a deep religious feeling.[13] Perhaps it was this last quality that made the Hanoverians favour clergymen's wives as wet nurses to the Royal Family.

The other test for this paragon of virtue was to examine the milk itself. Soranus of Ephesus, in the first century, had described the appearance of good milk, and suggested that the quality could best be evaluated by placing a drop on the fingernail. And this was still the only investigation available at the beginning of the nineteenth century apart, that is, from checking that it tasted sweet and had a pleasant smell. Parents were also advised that they should not take the nurse's word on trust, but should make certain, from time to time, that she was still producing milk, as some women would conceal the fact that their milk had dried up, for fear of losing their employment. After the nurse had fed their baby, parents should also ascertain that she had still more milk in her breasts, and they could get some idea of the volume that the child was getting if it had frequent wet nappies. But even here, the sly wet nurse had her tricks to conceal a lack of milk, for she would either secretly give the baby water before a feed, or pour water on its bedding, to hoodwink the unsuspecting parents.[14]

The problem was that, however detailed and attractive these descriptions of an ideal woman might be, when it came to finding one, it was often a compromise over the best that was available at the time. Mary Verney had such a problem in finding a suitable nurse during the Civil War. She finally wrote that she could only find Raph Rodes' wife, who was 'I feare—but poore and she looks like a slatterne but she sayeth if she takes the child she will have a mighty care of it,' and she added, 'truly she hathe two as fine children of her owne as ever I sawe'.[15] It is difficult to understand why she did not decide to keep the baby at home and feed him herself, under the circumstances, in view of her obvious concern for her son's welfare. Presumably, the practice of putting the baby out to nurse was so taken for granted, that this possibility was not even considered. At least, mothers like Mary Verney whose husband owned a large estate, would be likely to find a nurse from amongst their own tenants, who lived only a short distance away, and so could be visited quite often, while Royal or noble families customarily paid for the nurse to move into their own household. In such cases, the baby's health could be observed at close range, on a day to day basis, and any deterioration in its condition or care would quickly be noticed.

When Queen Anne gave birth to a son after seven pregnancies, which had all ended in miscarriage or death in early infancy, the choice of a wet nurse was clearly a matter of state importance. The young Prince was at first fed by Mrs Shermon, but he failed to thrive and eventually had a convulsion. Further attempts to find a nurse met with no success until a large reward was publicly advertised for a suitable mother.[16]We are told that wet nurses responded in droves, and Prince George, striding through an ante-chamber filled with such hopeful ladies, saw Mrs Pack with her month old son. He immediately took her to feed his child, and the baby Prince began to improve from that moment. She then became a woman of great importance and power, who must not be crossed under any circumstances, in case her milk should dry up and the young Prince be again put in peril of his life. For many recalled that Henrietta Maria, the wife of Charles I, had experienced a similar crisis when her Catholic wet nurse had refused to take the Oath of Allegiance. The resulting stress affected her milk, and the Royal family was thrown into turmoil, until another suitable woman could be found.[17]

However, under more favourable circumstances, the baby would be cared for by its wet nurse for two years or more. If the nurse lived in with her employer's family, she would be separated from her own husband and children for a long time. So, except in the case of very important families, it was more usual for the baby to be sent to live in its nurse's home for this peiod. And since it was recognised that babies did best when they were brought up in the heart of the country, rather than villages, like Kensington or Edmonton, which were closer to London, parents would have had little opportunity of visiting their baby during this time. Such enforced separation or 'putting out', as it was called, was condemned by Saint Bernardino in his sermons. He said that families would not know the child when it returned home several years later, saying 'I don't know who you are like—certainly none of us',[18] and William Buchan was also saddened by the lack of natural affection between parents and their offspring, when they had been separated for these critical years. Certainly, those who died at their nurse's home would have been strangers to their parents, who often did not go to the funeral. And Montaigne's comment that he had lost 'two or three at nurse, not without regret, but without grief' would have summed up many such parents' feelings.

But, apart from the well-to-do, who did not wish to feed their own children, there were of course women of all classes who could not manage to suckle their own babies due to illness. For them, and for all the infants of mothers who had died in childbirth, a substitute mother had to be found as soon as possible. Fortunately for Edward VI, when his mother died within a few weeks of his birth, he already had a wet nurse. In keeping with his status as heir to the throne, she was a well connected lady called Sybilla Penn, a sister-in-law to the Lord Chamberlain. She was probably closer to Edward than any Royal mother could ever have been, and totally devoted to his welfare. When he was eighteen months old, she carried him in her arms to meet the foreign Ambassadors, who had come to pay their respects to the young Prince. Overwhelmed by the strangeness of their manner and dress, he cried and hid his face in the folds of her gown. She stayed on, as his nanny, after he was weaned, and together with Will Somers, his father's jester, made up the little household that surrounded him at Hampton Court. She remained close to Edward all his short life, and was granted the Manor of Beamond in Buckinghamshire, in gratitude for her services.[19] Since Edward had never known his real mother, and was never separated from his foster mother, he was unusually fortunate to escape the conflict of loyalties and heartache that was so typical of babies that were wet nursed.

The final group of children for whom nurses were needed were those poor parish children, who had either been abandoned, in some cases because they were illegitimate, or who were orphaned. These babies were the responsibility of the parish in which they were born, and it was customary to put such infants out to foster mothers when they were very young. But for rich and poor babies alike, the homes of many of these wet nurses were often damp and draughty, and William Cadogan commented on the adverse effect of sending tiny babies from the stuffy oveheated atmosphere of the lying-in chamber to such places. In some cases a suitable mother would be found, who had recently delivered at the local work-house. Surprisingly, wealthy parents seem to have had no qualms about sending their own precious babies to join her in that insanitary institution, until such a time as she completed her lying-in, and returned to her own home.

The biggest problem, however, was the lack of supervision which such a system produced. The distance from the parental home ensured that the baby was unlikely to have regular visits from its mother and father, and owing to the short nature of most children's illnesses, the baby had often died before its parents learned that it was sick. It was common practice for nurses to dose their small charges with cordials containing opium, to keep them quiet, and in 1776, Dr Hume wrote that parents were often told that their child had died in convulsions when, in reality, it had succumbed to an overdose of this drug.[20] In some cases the parents may have been the victims of an even greater deceit. Guillemeau caustically referred to the belief that babies' personalities were 'changed at nurse', and said that they may well have been changed by an unscrupulous wet nurse who would conceal the death of her nursling, and substitute her own child in its stead. This would certainly have guaranteed the nurse's own child the very best possible start in life, way beyond her own limited means, and such a deception would not easily have been detected.

Such hazards had been recognised for a long time, and by the seventeenth century, the mortality rate of babies that were put out to nurse was becoming a national scandal. In 1653, Robert Pemell had criticised the practice of 'both high and low ladies, of farming out their babies to irresponsible women in the country.'[21] Beyond the reach of frequent checks, there is no doubt that some of these nurses would have substituted other food when they had difficulty in feeding the baby themselves, with disastrous results. Guil-lemeau recognised that any hired nurse would try to feed the baby on apples, pears, sops and 'such like trash' when she did not have enough milk. Yet the practice of putting out to nurse became ever more popular, as it spread from the wealthy to the middle classes, and then became a way of life for even the small tradesman's family. The Rector of Hayes, in Kent, told Doctor Walter Harris that when he had first come to his parish, it was filled with suckling infants from London, and at the end of the first year all but two had died. Since that time, the number of babies sent to professional nurses had been replaced twice over, yet he had buried every one of these infants before they were a year old.[22]

Nor was this practice confined to England. In 1780, the Chief of Police in Paris wrote that of the 21,000 infants born in Paris each year, less than 1,000 were breast fed by their mothers, and over 17,000 were sent to the country to be nursed.[23] Such was the traffic in these poor infants that in 1773 regulations were enacted to give the child a modicum of protection on its journey. The babies should always travel in the charge of a nurse, and the carts should have planked bottoms with a stated depth of fresh straw![24] But unlike the English, the Parisians found that babies that were sent to nurses living in the more affluent suburbs surrounding the Capital, did better than those who went further out into the villages of Normandy or Burgundy, and the rates of pay varied accordingly.

These babies usually stayed with their nurses until they were weaned, which in some cases was quite sudden. Up to this time the child's contact with its parents was likely to have been no more than a few half remembered visits from well-dressed strangers. By the time he returned to the family home, the infant would be eating an adult diet and walking unaided, and probably toilet trained, in most respects a miniature adult! Not suprisingly, there were considerable problems of readjustment on either side. The baby found itself taken from the only 'mother' that it had ever known, and expected to love a stranger. No wonder that Rousseau observed that the system was more likely to produce an ungrateful foster child than an affectionate son. Yet these problems, which seem so obvious and heartrending to us today, were by no means always appreciated. John Locke even wrote with approval, in *Some Thoughts Concerning Education*, of what he described as a prudent and kind mother of his acquaintance, who 'was forced to whip her little daughter, on her first coming home from nurse, eight times successively the same morning before she could master her stubbornness, and obtain her compliance in a very easy and indifferent matter'. When one realises that this little girl was probably under three years old, the confusion of feelings is pathetic, even when viewed across a distance of three centuries.

Wet nursing reached its zenith in the eighteenth century, when an increase in urban society made the system popular with all classes except the very poor. For if a mother decided that her infant should be put out to nurse, not only did she have someone to breast feed the baby, but at a stroke, she relieved herself of the whole burden of caring for the child for the next few years. At the same time, the pay and conditions of those nurses who were happy to 'live in' were far in excess of other domestic servants, and for many young women, the birth of an illegitimate baby was the door to a lucrative and fairly easy profession. No wonder it was sometimes spoken of as 'vice rewarded'.

But perhaps the saddest consequence of wet nursing was on the nurse's own child. Although a mother was sometimes found who had recently lost her own baby and was delighted to feed another, in most cases the nurse would stop feeding her own infant and give her milk to the foster child. This was normal practice, and an accepted part of the contract between the wet nurse and her employer. Things seem to have been managed better in France, where laws to control wet nursing had existed since the twelfth century, and where later legislation forbade a woman from taking on a stranger's child until her own was over nine months old. Although even these rules were often ignored by the middle of the nineteenth century. Ironically, it was about this time that Dr Budin of the Paris Maternité Hospital finally proved that it did not affect the quality of the milk if a mother fed more than one child at a time. In fact, if the baby was premature, or a poor feeder for some reason, then he regarded it as essential that she should nurse another vigorous infant as well, to keep the volume of milk high. For he observed that the amount of milk that was produced was dependent on the demand, and even the best nurse would dry up without the stimulus of strong suckling.[25]

He had his professional wet nurses successfully giving about thirty-four feeds a day, or about three pints of milk in all. Although he had observed that the supply seemed to be unlimited, he preferred to limit them to this quantity, as beyond this amount he detected signs of tiredness! They were exceptional ladies though, and much in demand by ordinary Parisian families, who would make a pretence of wishing to see the nursery arrangements at the Hospital, in order to entice away such well-endowed females to work for them. Dr Budin was furious to discover these deceptions taking place, and forbade the nurses to be present when the public was admitted on open days. Before he knew where he was, these formidable ladies were threatening to strike, and it needed a considerable amount of diplomacy and skill to return the atmosphere of his clinic to its usual placid tempo.

However, in spite of all his teaching, the traditional view that breast milk should not be shared, for fear of dilution, still held. Of course, wet nurses like Sybilla Penn, who was employed to feed the King's son, would arrange for another wet nurse to take care of her own child during this period. But poor mothers who became wet nurses to earn money for their families, could not afford to hire another woman, and their child was usually changed to hand feeding—with disastrous results.

William Buchan reckoned that not one child in a hundred survived after the mother had given her milk to another, and that consequently, the mother who was prepared to sacrifice her own child in this way, could not be a good mother to another's baby. Similar sentiments were expressed by the Countess of Lincoln, who in spite of employing wet nurses for all eighteen of her children, in her later years spoke out forcibly against the injustice of a system that demanded 'a poorer woman to banish her own infant for the entertaining of a richer woman's child'.

Although most parents do not seem to have had any qualms about the welfare of the wet nurse's own baby, there is a very poignant account from Benjamin Haydon, an eighteenth-century portrait painter, showing that at least one man had pangs of conscience over what he was doing. He had five children, all of whom died in infancy. When his daughter, Fanny, died he recorded in his diary that her whole lifespan had been no more than two years, nine months and twelve days. He went on to reflect that 'The life of this child has been one continued torture. She was weaned at three months from her Mother's weakness, and attempted to be brought up by hand. This failed, and she was reduced to a perfect skeleton. One day when I was kissing her, she sucked my cheek violently. I said "This child wants the bosom even now". Our medical Friend said it was an experiment, but we might try it. I got a wet nurse instantly, and she seized the bosom like a tigress; in a few months she recovered, but the woman who came to suckle her weaned her own child.

'I called on the nurse before she came, and found a fine baby, her husband and herself in great poverty. I said "What do you do with this child?" She replied "Wean it sir. We *must* do so, we are *poor!*" I went away. "Is it just" thought I "to risk the life of another child to save my own?" I went home in tortured feelings of what to do, but a desire to save my own predominated.

'The nurse came, Fanny was saved, but the fine baby of the poor nurse paid the penalty. I was never easy. "Fanny never can and never will prosper" I imagined. What right had I to take advantage of the poverty of this poor woman to save my own child, when I found out she had an infant? I ought not to have had her. In spite of my reason I did have her and though my own Child was saved for the time, I always felt it would be but justice if my child too in the end became the sacrifice to the Manes of the child which had died in consequence of its Mother's leaving it.'[26]

But although wet nursing died out in England with the advent of safer bottle feeding, as the diminishing number of advertisements for wet nurses during the course of the nineteenth century demonstrated, it continued in other parts of Europe until later. And today it still persists in large maternity hospitals, albeit in a rather more disembodied form. Breast milk is donated by mothers who have more than enough for their own babies' needs, to a central bank where it is pasteurised and used to feed premature and sickly infants. For, in spite of all the recent advances in infant feeding, breast is still best!

1 'Birth of the Virgin' by Israhel van Meckenem.
This depicts the activities in a lying-in chamber in medieval times. The nurse is testing the water's temperature with her heel, while the cradle, with its safety bands already in place, awaits the swaddled baby. In the background a servant hangs up the swaddling bands to dry.

2 'Birth of the Virgin' by Giotto.
In the foreground a nurse pinches the baby's nose into shape, whilst
beside her another woman rolls up a swaddling band.

3 *Above:* An engraving which shows how the lungs of an apparently lifeless baby could be inflated by means of a small tube and bellows.

4 *Right:* An incubator, or *couveuse*, at Dr Budin's clinic in Paris. The box was warmed by hot water bottles that were placed underneath it. The baby is about to be placed in the *couveuse* wearing 'ordinary swaddling clothes' and the glass cover will then be placed on top of the incubator.

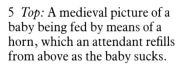

5 *Top:* A medieval picture of a baby being fed by means of a horn, which an attendant refills from above as the baby sucks.

6 *Centre:* A simple breast pump that could be operated by the mother. Illustration from Omnibonus Ferrarius *De Arte Medica Infantium*, 1577.

7 *Right:* Hugh Smith's Bubby Pot.

8 'Nursing Twins' by Pieter Gerritsz van Roestraten.
The twin in the foreground is being spoon fed from a small dish. The
nurse's cane seat would be hung on the wall when not in use.

9 *Above:* 'Visit to the Child at Nurse' by George Moreland. In this engraving the elegantly dressed mother and her older child have come to visit their baby. The infant clings to the wet nurse, no doubt bewildered by these 'unknown' visitors. The two older children are probably the nurse's own family.

10 *Opposite:* Painting of a fifteen-week-old baby holding a wooden feeding bottle, dated 1593.

11 *Right:* A sucking bottle of similar design but made of pewter.

Año Dñi . 15 93   Ætatis Suæ. 15. Sep.

DAIRY IN GOLDEN LANE, CITY

12 *Top:* An illustration from Sadler's *Infant Feeding by Artificial Means*, showing direct suckling from asses. Fortunately, the animals would appear to be very docile.

13 *Bottom:* A City dairy in Golden Lane, 1835.
The cows are seen behind the pen at the back of the shop. Hay was probably stored in the cellar after it was unloaded through the hatch under the window.

4

How Shall we Feed the Baby?

What did a mother do in the past when she could not breast feed her baby, or arrange for a wet nurse to do it for her? Some sort of substitute food had to be devised, but with no knowledge of the essential constituents of breast milk, it was not surprising that the results were often fatal. In fact, the success rate was so poor that this hand feeding, as it was called, did not merit any serious considerations by doctors until the eighteenth century. But there is plenty of evidence that it went on before this. Feeding bottles that were discovered in infants' graves from the pre-Christian era suggest that the practice may have been common amongst the Greeks and Romans, and such a feeding bottle that was found in France dates back to 2,000 years BC.[1] The coming of Christianity brought to an end this custom of burying a child with its valued earthly possessions, but a medieval picture in the Wellcome Museum clearly shows a swaddled baby being fed from a hollowed out cow's horn. And feeding a new-born baby animal milk was certainly a possibility in sixteenth-century Scotland. When a midwife was begged by a newly delivered mother to take her illegitimate child away with her, she replied that she could do nothing for the bairn, as she had 'neither woman's milk or cow's milk to give it'.[2]

In 1688, the King's physicians actually chose to hand feed the long awaited son of James II and his wife, Mary of Modena.[3] This policy would not appear to have been unique for, according to a contemporary French diplomat, many babies were brought up in this manner in England. In this case the decision was taken because all but one of the royal couple's previous children had

died while being wet nursed. Although initially the little Prince
seemed to thrive on a strict diet that consisted of little more than
boiled water, cereals and sugar, by seven weeks of age it was clear
that he was dying from what was described as 'colic dysentery and
similar disorders'. At this point the anxious King brought the
whole exercise rapidly to a close by sending to the nearest village
for a wet nurse to feed the baby and the famished child recovered.
Later the Queen wrote that the state that her son was reduced to
by 'this fine experiment' would deter her from ever allowing it to
be tried on the children of others.

   Although it is understandable that the royal physicians were not
keen to write about the details of this regime which had nearly led
to the death of the heir to the throne, it is significant that the
problems of hand feeding had defeated some of the best medical
minds in the kingdom. And it is not until almost a century later
that we find one or two physicians who were prepared to admit the
possibility of successful hand feeding from birth, to their readers.
Even so, it was still regarded as something of a minor miracle to
bring up a baby from birth by such methods. And when Pip, in
Dickens' *Great Expectations* spoke of his older sister, Mrs
Gargery, he recalled that she had established a great reputation for
herself with her neighbours, when she managed to bring him up
'by hand'. For although there were instances of success with hand
feeding, whether or not any individual baby survived seemed to be
largely a matter of chance, and until the end of the nineteenth
century, this would have been the generally accepted view of hand
feeding.

   It is not really suprising that the problem of finding a substitute
for breast milk should have proved so daunting, since even well
educated parents would have had only the vaguest notions of their
baby's needs. The likeliest replacement was animal milk—on the
grounds that what was clearly very good for the calf or kid, should
be sufficient for the human infant. Cow's milk was probably the
easiest to obtain, and until Elizabethan times, even a city the size
of London was never more than ten minutes' walk from the
surrounding countryside, where fresh milk could be bought.[4] But
cow's milk is not ideal for the very young infant, since it contains
too much protein and mineral salts, and not enough sugar or
vitamin C by comparison with human milk. So even though it

seems to have been common practice to dilute it with water, and to add a little sugar or honey, mothers still regarded this modified milk as inferior to that of goats or donkeys, which was more easily digested by the tiny baby. Ass's milk was thought most closely to resemble breast milk, as it produced the smallest curd, and it was always recommended for invalids and very young or frail babies. This was not always easy to find and as late as 1857, the British Pharmacoepia, in all seriousness, suggested that a passable imitation could be made by boiling up vineyard snails with pearl barley![5] And since fresh ass's milk was almost twice the price of ordinary milk, it was quite common for the donkey to be brought to the house by a dairyman and milked on the doorstep, so that the purchaser would have no doubts of its origin or freshness.[6]

For fresh milk was critical to the success of hand feeding. While London was still small enough for the family to walk to an outlying farm for its supplies, there was hope of success. But without the help of pasteurisation, this unrefrigerated milk would have gone sour in a matter of hours. Of course, this had always been appreciated, and the sale of milk was allowed on a Sunday—a special privilege that was only accorded to milk and mackerel.[7] With the expansion of the capital in the seventeenth and eighteenth centuries, it was no longer possible for most Londoners to buy their milk directly from a farm, and they became dependent on middle men for its distribution. Some of these supplies continued to be brought into the City from nearby farms, and no doubt on a warm day got hotter and more lethal at every turn in the journey. But there were few profits to be made from sour milk, and many town dairymen preferred to keep their cows in stables close to their premises, where they could be milked as required, although, with no access to grazing land, or even daylight in some cases, the quality of this milk must have been very poor. Some idea of the conditions in such establishments was given in *The Lancet* in 1855. It described a dairy in Clerkenwell, where thirty to forty cows were kept in a disgusting state, their legs full of ulcers and their teats diseased. Similarly, forty cows kept at the Adelphi Arches were all found to have the mange.[8] This was not altogether surprising, when we learn that they were stabled in cellars and never saw the light of day! As time went on, the needs of London's growing population meant that the demand for fresh milk always outstripped the supply, and it was not until the development of the railway network in the second half of the nineteenth century that a satisfactory method of distribution to towns became possible.

The best milk to be found in London before this was probably from the small herds in the Royal Parks, where methods of collection and cleanliness would have been reasonable, but this milk was expensive. The poor had to make do with cheaper stuff of very uncertain origin and quality. For by the eighteenth century, there was a relative scarcity of milk in London and the South of England generally, since the Enclosure Acts had done away with much of the common land on which a cottager could graze a cow. As a result there was a great temptation for dairies to cheat their customers, and they were notorious for deliberately thinning the milk with water, and then adding chalk to make it appear creamy again. Even the lactometer, which was used to check the quality of the milk, could be fooled, for the unscrupulous dairyman, to avoid a suspiciously low reading after the water had been added, would first remove some of the cream as well![9] When this cheaper milk, collected under filthy conditions, had been skimmed, diluted with unboiled chalky water, and then carted round London in dirty containers, it is amazing that any poor baby survived the first days of life after being fed this noxious brew. In fact, the evidence of contemporary writers suggests that few infants did, and it was only those who had the good fortune to be brought up in the country, or whose families could afford clean milk, that had any hope of success with hand feeding.

But having decided to feed animal milk to her baby, the mother then had the problem of finding a suitable bottle or container that the new born baby could suck. The easiest solution, of course, was to put the baby to an animal to suck directly, and this seems to have been practised quite frequently, as the legendary story of Romulus and Remus would suggest. Although not popular in England, it was common in France, and in 1775, Alphonse Le Roy wrote of the Foundling Institution in Aix, where babies were nourished by goats in this way. He described how 'each goat which comes to feed, enters bleating into the ward, and goes to hunt the infant which has been given to it, pushes back the covering with its horns and straddles the crib to give suck to the infant'.[10] At least this milk would have been clean and fresh, and this probably accounted for the reputed success of the method, which was still recommended as late as 1896 in Sadler's account of *Infant Feeding by Artificial Means.* And this book contained several fascinating illustrations of babies being fed in this manner by both goats and donkeys.

If direct feeding from the animal was not a practical possibility, then some sort of container had to be devised. Probably the cow's horn was the simplest to obtain, and with its core removed, and a small hole at its tip, it could easily be transformed into a makeshift feeder. George Armstrong, the eighteenth-century physician, who founded the first dispensary for children, gave details of the method.[11] Having obtained a suitable horn that would hold about four to five ounces of fluid, a finger stall, made of parchment or soft leather, was tied around its perforated end and when the baby sucked, the milk would seep through the gaps between the stitches. Such a container had several obvious advantages, it was simple and cheap to make, and due to its open ended design, the baby would have to drink all its milk in one go. And a medieval picture of such a feed suggests that an attendant may have been needed to top it up from above, as the baby sucked.

Unlike the horn, the bottle once filled could be left half full between feeds, and in a warm room would rapidly have gone sour. Many of the ancient bottles were made of pottery, but in the Colchester Castle Museum there is one that is made of glass that dates from Roman times. By the seventeenth century the variety of design was enormous, and the materials that were used ranged from wood to pewter, usually with a removable top which resembled a teat, which the baby would attempt to suck. All of them presented problems of cleanliness, the innermost recesses of these early bottles must have teemed with bacteria that would guarantee to send any baby to the grave. For although medical writers did suggest that the mother should rinse out the bottle after use, the importance of scrupulous cleanliness as a prerequisite for safe hand feeding was not appreciated. And the problem of providing a teat did not help. All sorts of ideas were used with varying results, from stuffing a small piece of linen cloth with a sponge, through which the milk would filter, to tying on a pickled heifer's teat! But until the arrival of the india rubber teat with Elijah Pratt's patent in 1845, there was nothing that could successfully control the volume of flow, and be easily cleaned.[12]

For the frail baby, spoon feeding was often of help, but it was slow and tedious, and for all infants there was the further problem of deciding just how much food the baby needed each day. By the late eighteenth century, Hugh Smith's suggestion of a pint of milk a day for the new born baby, rising to two pints, at three months of age, was a surprisingly accurate estimate. But even after this time there was no general agreement, and when in doubt, parents tended to stuff their child with large volumes of food, especially if he did not appear to be thriving on cow's milk.

For, as Hugh Smith recognised, the commonest cause of death amongst this group of hand fed infants was diarrhoea, or the 'watery gripes' as it was known, which would carry a small baby off in a matter of days. This infection, often transmitted by dirty milk, was too much for very young babies, and with no means of correcting the dehydration caused by the resulting diarrhoea and vomiting, the baby would rapidly succumb. Of course, it was not until a century later that the bacterial cause of these illnesses was recognised, and it is easy to see how in the eighteenth century it appeared that liquid food such as animal milk, led to liquid stools—and to prevent this diarrhoea, many reasoned that the milk should be thickened with flour or bread, or even eliminated altogether, in favour of more solid food. If the baby appeared to be ailing, parents were tempted to give it as much food as possible, and Hugh Smith complained that they would not believe him when he said that there was more nutriment in a pint of cow's milk than a quart of bread sops. He was ahead of his time in his appreciation of the food value of milk, and not all doctors agreed with him. Even George Armstrong believed that the smallest of babies would need a huge volume if it were to survive on milk alone, and that consequently such a large amount of 'thin' liquid would be very likely to lead to diarrhoea. For this reason he preferred that the child should be fed from a spoon or pap boat— so that the milk could be thickened with bread and other foods.

If animal milk was not used as a replacement for breast feeding, then attempts would be made to produce a substitute food for the baby from other ingredients. Lacking any detailed analysis of the essential elements of breast milk, the mother would try to make this pap or panada, as it was called, resemble breast milk in its physical appearance, in the hope that she was thereby reproducing its other qualities. Pap was usually made by adding water or milk, or a mixture of both, to bread or flour. A little sugar was then added, together with a variety of other ingredients, including on occasions Castile soap which was thought to aid digestion! Most of the nourishment in such mixtures came from its milk content, and in many cases only water was added to the flour or bread, a result that Dr Richard Conyers, a physician to the Foundling Hospital, wisely observed was good for sticking books together, but would not support a child, even for one day. He suggested that parents could estimate its nutritional value by seeing how a grown man fared on such a diet! The baby's inevitable hunger usually led to crying, and the poor child would be given still more of the sticky stuff until he was too bloated or exhausted to cry further. According to Hugh Smith, who deplored the practice of giving any pap to new born babies, often as much as a quart of such food was given in twenty-four hours.

Since pap was thicker than milk, it could not be given through a horn or bottle, and the nurse would need to use a spoon or pap boat instead. These little dishes resembled gravy boats without a handle, and were normally made of china, although wealthier families would have them in silver. Spoons were often specially adapted for their task and would have a hollow stem so that the nurse could blow the pap down the baby's throat for an even faster—and no doubt, larger, feed. It was to avoid such forced feeding that Hugh Smith invented his own baby feeder, which he called the Bubby Pot, designed so that the infant had to suck up every bit of his food and, according to the wise doctor, labour for his supper instead of having it poured down his throat whether he wanted it or not.

In practice, most parents would seem to have used a combination of animal milk and pap in their attempts to find a substitute for breast milk. Probably for careful parents, who had access to fresh milk, there was hope of success, always providing of course, that the baby was healthy to start with, but for the majority of poor infants the likelihood of succeeding was still as precarious as it had ever been. For according to Dr Buchan, not one baby in a hundred survived when it was hand fed, and he was not prepared to discuss even the possibility of successful hand feeding with his readers. And it is significant that when the Governors of the Foundling Hospital asked the advice of the Royal College of Physicians as to the possibility of hand feeding some of their babies, the decision was made to send them all to wet nurses. For although careful and devoted parents might successfully raise one child at a time, under good conditions, when it came to feeding many children in an institution, the chances of survival were negligible, and the Dublin Foundling Hospital which hand fed over 10,000 infants in the twenty-one years between 1775 and 1796, had only forty-five survivors—a staggering 99.6% mortality rate![13]

Yet by the late eighteenth century, at least two doctors were prepared to consider the possibility of successful hand feeding, if breast milk was not available. Although Hugh Smith blamed the high infant mortality in London on this artificial feeding, he still preferred it to employing a wet nurse, and devoted a section of his book to details of the method he believed to be safest. He insisted that the cow's milk should be boiled for the first two months of a baby's life, and a little sugar added, to make it taste as sweet as breast milk. After three months unboiled milk should be given, and at the same time other items of food, such as broths and chicken meat, should be introduced into the diet. For he argued that animal milk was not as complete a food as breast milk for the baby, and needed such supplements to be as nourishing. George Armstrong agreed that animal milk should be boiled unless the parents were sure of its freshness. He wrote with personal experience of the problems, for as he told his readers, he had successfully hand reared his own two children, when their mother's milk failed.

It is interesting that although they were ignorant of the real cause for failure with hand feeding, by the late eighteenth century, a fairly successful empirical method had been worked out. No doubt the boiling of milk for the first two months of the baby's life would have given it considerable protection against infantile diarrhoea, at its most vulnerable age. And although this heating would also have destroyed much of the valuable vitamin content as well, the introduction of unboiled milk together with other foods at three months, would probably have prevented the appearance of frank vitamin deficiency later.

By the 1840s, successful attempts were being made to preserve cow's milk, and the condensed and evaporated milks that came onto the market at this time were very popular, especially with the poor. Mothers found themselves no longer dependent on the unscrupulous and dishonest dairyman for their supplies—for the sterility of the milk, and in the case of condensed milk its excellent keeping qualities, made it appear superior to the fresh variety. The success of these products encouraged more women, especially poor working mothers, to abandon breast feeding in their favour. Sadly, they were mistaken in thinking that these were as good as the breast, for they were often made from skimmed milk, and contained very little Vitamin C or D. Not surprisingly, babies that were fed exclusively on these canned milks, although appearing to thrive initially, soon developed signs of scurvy and rickets. And by 1870, one third of the children who lived in industrial cities, such as Manchester or London, were found to have clinical rickets.[14]

Milk had also been preserved by drying, and in this powdered form had been available from the middle of the century, although due to problems of manufacture, it had never been as popular as condensed or evaporated milk. But like all cow's milk, it contained relatively little Vitamin C in comparison with breast milk, and half of this was lost in the drying process. Just why these preserved milks were so unsatisfactory for newborn babies was to remain a mystery until 1906, when Gowland Hopkins put forward the hypothesis that small quantities of vital amines were essential for good nutrition. When it was realised that cow's milk was probably deficient, then mothers were advised to make sure that alternative sources were available in the bottle fed baby's diet. From this time onwards, the prospects for successful hand feeding steadily improved, although even then it was not until the 1930s that it became possible to fortify these dried milks directly with vitamins during their manufacture, to bring them up to breast milk levels.

But by the early 1970s it became clear that such milk products were so successful that Britain, in the terms of a 1974 report on infant feeding, was fast becoming a bottle fed nation.[15] A survey showed that only 50% of first time mothers attempted to breast feed, and many of these gave up soon after they left hospital. This was worrying because, in spite of the good results with bottle feeding, there was still no doubt that breast milk was the best food for the newborn baby.

Commercial milk powders were still made from cow's milk and although they had been modified to resemble human milk, there remained a significant difference between the two. The protein and mineral content was higher in the formula milk and their fat was not so easily digested by small babies. Many of these feeds were difficult to make up. Some required the addition of extra sugar, while a variety of measuring scoops and containers caused further confusion so that the reconstituted feed was often too concentrated. In such cases a small baby was likely to become dangerously dehydrated, particularly if an attack of vomiting or diarrhoea had already depleted its body fluid. And the high mineral content of these feeds could seriously overload a premature baby's kidneys. While even if they were lucky enough to avoid these early problems, there was evidence that such concentrated feeds and the early introduction of solids was leading to an increase in childhood obesity.

So recommendations were made that the importance of breast feeding should be stressed to all prospective parents, and that the proprietary milk powders should be further modified to resemble breast milk more closely. And to simulate breast feeding still further, mothers should be encouraged to give their baby its bottle 'on demand' and not at fixed times, while either breast feeding or formula milk should be given for the first six months of life until the infant's digestive system had matured sufficiently to cope with ordinary cow's milk.

By the time that the second survey was made in 1980, it was clear that many of the earlier recommendations had been implemented. Greater public awareness of the importance of breast feeding had led to nearly 70% of first time mothers breast feeding their babies, and many continued for four months or more. The baby food manufacturers had quickly responded to the suggestions for improvement and the new milk products were much nearer to breast milk in their composition. At the same time it appeared that many parents were heeding the warnings about the early introduction of solids and delaying until their baby was three or more months old.

Not only had the manufacturers changed the composition of their products, but they had also standardised the scoops for measuring the powder so that this potential source of error in reconstituting a feed was eliminated. And because they had made the formula complete, the mother no longer had to add anything but boiling water, which reduced the danger of contaminating the milk.

The importance of sterility in preparing milk feeds for small babies had only been proved scientifically just over a hundred years earlier. Pasteur had demonstrated not only that micro-organisms were responsible for the putrefaction of food, but that these micro-organisms could be prevented from multiplying in raw milk by heating it to sixty-five degrees centigrade for thirty minutes and then cooling it rapidly. Ironically, this improvement was first appreciated by farmers and dairymen, who were encouraged to find that it prolonged the 'shelf life' of fresh milk.[16] Pasteurisation, as this process was called, was initially introduced in 1890 for commercial reasons, and it was only after its introduction that it became clear that such treated milk was also safer for the consumer. For all the potentially harmful bacteria were destroyed by pasteurisation, including the bacteria that caused tuberculosis. This discovery, that tuberculosis was caused by infection, and that children often contracted the disease by drinking contaminated milk, proved at last, if further proof were needed, that wholesome milk was essential to the success of hand feeding. Parents were urged to make certain that their children's milk came from herds that had been declared free from the disease. Yet, in spite of these improvements, it was still common for milk to be sold directly from a churn, and a measure was poured into any container that the family had to hand. Dairymen would often offer children a drink from a ladle, and this was replaced, uncleaned, in the churn for the next customer. It was not until the 1920s that milk that had been bottled under hygienic conditions was generally available.

Before this time, there had been many attempts to set up centres for the distribution of safe milk for small babies who were most at risk from contaminated milk. The idea of such a centre seems to have originated with Dr Pierre Budin's clinic in Paris, some forty years earlier. He achieved remarkable results by seeing his babies on a weekly basis, and those who were hand fed were given bottles of sterilised milk, that were each sufficient for one feed.[17] Even though this milk cannot have been ideal, the babies seem to have flourished under his close supervision and care. His example inspired the setting up of similar distribution centres on this side of the channel. Such voluntary societies mushroomed during the First World War, in response to the needs of poor families in wartime, and when the war ended, they were to form the basis of the Infant Welfare Clinics, where mothers could receive, in addition to good quality milk, free help and guidance on all aspects of their babies' health and progress.

Considering how little was known of a small baby's needs, and the difficulties that were involved, it is amazing that any infants survived hand feeding from birth, before the present century. Yet a lucky few did manage to avoid the enteritis transmitted by contaminated food, and to overcome the problems caused by an inadequate diet. But such survivors were relatively few, and as late as 1870, over 33% of hand fed babies were reckoned to die within the first year of life.[18] Part of the reason for this failure had been suspected by Sir Richard Conyers, more than a hundred years earlier, when he observed that when cow's milk was boiled, its most subtle part was destroyed—but no such changes appeared to occur in warm milk from the mother's breast.[19] However, it was not until the scientific discoveries of the twentieth century that it was possible to explain why this was so, and for the first time to devise a substitute for breast milk that was both safe and nutritious.

5

Weaning and the Perils of Teething

Even if their child appeared to be thriving on breast milk, the most optimistic of parents would view the next step—the introduction of an adult diet—with considerable trepidation. For at any time during this changeover period a previously healthy infant might go into a decline, and once started, this deterioration in health was extremely difficult to reverse. Understandably, there was no end to the variety of advice on weaning, but orthodox medical opinion, since Galen's time, had held that the arrival of the first tooth was the surest sign that the baby was capable of digesting more solid food. This should be introduced slowly over a period of about eighteen months, and only when the last of the milk teeth had erupted would it be safe to stop breast feeding altogether.

For children were thought to die from the effects of teething, the underlying cause of which was probably a vitamin deficiency, due to an inadequate diet. But in the centuries before vitamins were discovered, teething itself was thought to be the cause, and this explained the apprehension with which the whole lengthy process was anticipated. Such anxiety was evident when Lady Bryan wrote of her charge, the young Princess Elizabeth, 'God knoweth my Lady hath great pain with her teeth, and they come very slowly forth—which causeth me to suffer her Grace to have her will more than I would',[1] and Hugh Smith pointed out that once the danger of death from diarrhoea had been accounted for, the commonest cause of death in young children came from teething. And so serious were these problems, that 40% of *all* deaths in the seventeenth century were found to occur in children under the age of two years.[2] In fact, the Bills of Mortality devoted a special section to deaths below this age, and it is significant that this was the period of time that the milk teeth usually took to erupt. But although the problems of teething seem to have reached almost epidemic proportions at this time, they were not a recent phenomenon, and had been known to Hippocrates. All descriptions of the Breeding of Teeth, as this condition was called, gave much the same picture—of a distressed baby suffering great pain from swollen and haemorrhagic gums, and finally dying of a fever or in convulsions. In many cases the symptoms came on as early as five months of age, in which case the baby was unlikely to live to see its first birthday! Conversely, it was generally agreed that the later the symptoms appeared, the more hope there was of the child's eventual recovery. And few would have quarrelled with Robert Pemell when he said that of all the afflictions of childhood, none was more grievous than teething.

In retrospect, it would seem that the likeliest cause of these troubles was the premature weaning from breast milk before the baby had had a chance to adapt completely to an adult diet. St Augustine had warned parents of such dangers and told them to 'be fearful lest anyone be weaned from milk before his time' and added that should a weakling in his earliest infancy be deprived of milk, he would surely perish.[3] Yet even though Galen had taught that nothing but breast milk should be given until the first tooth had erupted, it would seem to have been fairly common, even in medieval times, for the weaning process to be started earlier, often at no more than three months of age, and Bartholomew the Englishman referred to the nurse chewing food for the 'toothless babe'.[4] She should roll up little pills of bread, soften them with her saliva, and then pop them into the baby's mouth. Other articles of food were treated in the same way, but first she should chew them well, so that they were reduced to a sort of purée, before giving them to her charge. This practice was actually regarded as one of the nurse's duties, and only one writer, Simon de Vallembert, condemned it, on the grounds that it might give the child worms.

As the infant grew and its appetite increased, so larger pieces of bread would be mashed up in a little milk or water, and when this was given to the baby before it was put to the breast, the subsequent demand for breast milk was reduced. No doubt this would have come as a relief to many undernourished mothers, for it was noted that 'because of their continual labour and poor life, these mothers do not have a lot of milk, so that they would not be capable of feeding a child if he did not take other nourishment in addition to milk from the breast'.[5] And country women, who were expected to work in the fields all day, would have found it difficult to return home every few hours to suckle their babies, and in such cases this pap would be given as a substitute for their mothers' milk. By such means, we are told, they could go for long hours between feeds. But although such food might fill a hungry baby's stomach for a while, in comparison to breast milk, its nutritional value was small.

Even though Jacques Guillemeau reiterated the importance of waiting for the first tooth before weaning, by the seventeenth century, the early introduction of pap seems to have become commonplace to rich and poor babies alike. De Vallembert had suggested that an egg yolk could be added to these mixtures, but in the majority of cases only bread and water seems to have been given, and it is not surprising that babies that were brought up on this sort of diet soon showed signs of malnutrition.

However, the well-nourished baby would probably have cut his first tooth at about six months of age. If this had come earlier, it would have been welcomed as a propitious sign, for Thomas Phaire pointed out that the sooner the teeth appeared, the easier the whole business was likely to be. And when the Dauphin, later Louis XIII, ran a fever and cried all night, at seven months of age, his personal physician, Dr Jean Héroard, sat by his cradle and held his hand to comfort him. Fortunately, his misery was short lived, and two days later the child's dresser found that the tooth had erupted. The apothecary was sent post haste to Fontainebleau, to tell the King the good news as soon as possible.[6] So important was this event in the life of the child, that parents often held a small party to celebrate its arrival, and gave a thank-you present to the wet nurse,[7] while the baby would receive a coral stick to act as a teething ring. Coral was thought to have magical properties, and was frequently combined with a silver rattle as a useful toy for the young infant. Should the child be threatened by a serious illness, it was said to go pale, and such coral sticks may be seen hanging round the necks of young children in portraits of the seventeenth century.

Once the first tooth had arrived, the baby's diet became more varied, and chewing on a chicken bone would encourage the other teeth to erupt with the minimum of bother and distress. Meats and broths were also introduced, together with vegetables, providing that they were well cooked. For it was thought that maggots that were to be found in fruit and vegetables were the source of worms in children, and it was only safe to give these foods to babies if they had been boiled for a very long time. Animal milk, and later small beer, would gradually replace breast milk, and weaning was finally completed with the arrival of the last of the milk teeth. But even then, caution was urged, and some writers advised parents that it was better to wait for the autumn rather than attempt to finish weaning in summer, when the dangers of summer diarrhoea were at their height. Likewise, any attempts to complete weaning during the rigours of winter were unwise when other fresh food was in short supply, and it was better to wait for the spring.[8] If things could be so arranged that the final feed was given when there was a full moon—and on Good Friday—then parents could rest content that they had chosen the most auspicious time for the completion of this worrying and hazardous task.[9]

By the time the child had reached three years of age, it would be eating the same food as its parents, with one important exception—there was unlikely to have been much fresh fruit in its diet, as this was thought to be harmful to babies and young children. There were several reasons for this attitude. The Humoral Doctrine, on which the whole theory of medieval medicine was based, had said that all of God's creation was made up of four elements— air, fire, earth and water, and man was divided into one of four types, depending on the preponderance of these elements in his make-up. Illness was thought to occur when this balance was upset, and could be corrected by avoiding foods of the wrong type. So it was particularly unfortunate that babies and toddlers were in the group that was forbidden fruit.

Although the validity of this theory was later to be questioned, the prejudice against fruit remained. Even adults were wary of eating too much fruit, since it was thought to cause fevers, and its sale was actually banned in the streets of London in 1569, when pestilence threatened, and later, during the Plague, gooseberries, melons and cherries were particularly suspect.[10] Part of this fear may have been due to the natural laxative effect of ripe fruit when eaten in large amounts, and since such symptoms were most likely to occur in summer, when fruit was plentiful, it is easy to see how this could be confused with infantile diarrhoea, which was so dreaded. When parents also found maggots in some of this fruit, which resembled the little threadworms that were common in children, then even the most open-minded of them would have found it difficult to argue against this ban. Mrs Sharpe would only allow children to eat oranges and pomegranates, because these fruits never had maggots, and the popularity of orangeries during the Stuart period may have been partly due to the orange's apparent safety in this respect.

But even though doctors advised that fruit was unsuitable for young children, there is visual evidence that in some families it was available in the nursery, and the painting of 'The Cobham Family' shows the younger Cobhams tucking into plates of fruit and nuts with their elders. And, no doubt, poor children would have eaten all that they could get, without worrying unduly about the theories of the medical men, for it was said that they did not know what it was to follow a diet, being obliged to eat everything that they had,[11] while children that were brought up in the country would have had easy access to all types of fruit, without much supervision. Nevertheless, town dwellers who were worried about their children's health, and wealthy enough to consult a physician, would have been advised to avoid all fresh fruit and uncooked vegetables—and it was amongst the children of well-to-do London families that the problems of malnutrition were most marked.

Of course, we now know that fruit and green vegetables are a good source of Vitamin C so it was particularly unfortunate that fruit was often forbidden to children, while the prolonged boiling of vegetables would inevitably have destroyed much of their vitamin content. When growing children were deprived of such useful sources of Vitamin C they were very likely to develop scurvy.

The effects of this disease had been known for centuries, and it was at its most florid in sailors, who went on long sea voyages without access to fresh food. Within weeks they would show signs of the deficiency, and would become lethargic with noticeably swollen limbs. Mysterious bruises would appear on their bodies, and their gums would bleed. It was recognised that a similar condition occurred in land dwellers, particularly at the end of a long hard winter, when little fresh food was available, and all the meat was salted. By the sixteenth century, mariners in the west knew of a variety of cures, ranging from lemon juice to green herbs—but the cause was still undiscovered, although it was usually thought to be connected with salt. For the condition rapidly improved when fresh meat was eaten again, and sailors who lived and worked in a salty atmosphere and ate a great deal of salted meat, exhibited the worst aspects of the disease. And it was for this reason that children were forbidden to add salt to their food.

But scurvy not only has an effect on the gums of adults—in babies the gums become swollen and haemorrhagic. These, of course, were just the symptoms that occurred in the worst cases of teething, and there seems little doubt, from contemporary accounts, that scurvy was at least partly responsible for these problems. Strangely, the possibility that such symptoms in small babies might be related to scurvy does not seem to have been postulated, but Gideon Harvey did recognise that scurvy was to be found in older children, and he suggested that it was an infection that was spread by parents kissing their children. It seems to have been so prevalent in the capital in the seventeenth century that he described scurvy as the Disease of London.

Another likely cause of these teething difficulties was rickets. This condition was described by Daniel Whistler in 1645, and he claimed that it had first been seen in England some twenty-six years earlier.[12] Whether this really was a new disease is open to doubt, for evidence of rickets has been found in skeletons dating back to the first century. But before its separate identity was recognised, it may well have been confused with scurvy, since both were likely to have occurred together when the baby's diet was inadequate. In Whistler's thesis, which was published in Leyden, he wrote of the effects of rickets on the growing baby's bones, and the characteristic bowing of the legs which was noticeable when the child began to stand. He observed that in such cases, teething was also likely to be delayed. The cause was a mystery, but lack of exercise and a 'dull environment' were suspected of having a lot to do with it.

Nowadays, rickets is known to be due to a deficiency of Vitamin D. Large quantities of this vitamin are available in milk and dairy products and some fish liver oils, but, unlike Vitamin C it can also be made in the body, providing there is an adequate supply of calcium in the diet, and the child is exposed to sunlight for a few hours each day. While the fully breast fed baby would have been protected from both rickets and scurvy, when the supply of this milk was limited, and the infant's hunger satisfied with bread pap, then a deficiency of both vitamins was very likely to occur. Also, since the swaddled baby even had its face covered for protection when it was taken out into the fresh air, it was unlikely to have made much Vitamin D of its own, in the first few months of life.

Such well-intentioned cossetting could only have added to the baby's problems, and it is interesting that by the seventeenth century, rickets was known as a condition that visited 'the cradles of the rich'.[13] When Charles I came to London from Scotland on the accession of his father, he had marked signs of the disease. So much so that King James was anxious for him to wear a special pair of iron boots, which he hoped would prevent his son's legs from bending,[14] and this little pair of boots can still be seen in the Museum of London. Charles was slow to walk, and was still being carried by a servant at four years of age. But apart from specially strengthened boots and rigid corsets, doctors had little to offer in the way of treatment for the bony deformities caused by rickets.

It seems strange that although the effects of scurvy and rickets were well recognised in adult and older children, the possibility that these conditions might also affect small babies in some way does not seem to have been considered. When a baby was obviously distressed by teething, its parents felt powerless to help. But although they were ignorant of the real cause of these problems, they were nevertheless well aware that once they made their appearance, their child was in mortal danger. Ambrose Paré, the sixteenth-century French surgeon, wrote of a father who had asked him to examine the body of his eight month old son, in an effort to find the cause of his mysterious death from teething. Paré dissected beneath the swollen gums, and found all the teeth lying in perfect array. He bewailed the fact that the father had not called him in earlier, when he might have saved the child's life by cutting the gums to let the teeth erupt.[15] This was fairly desperate treatment, but lancing did seem to have had some success, and doctors recorded instances where such action was followed by an almost miraculous cure. Perhaps the fuller diet, which would have followed on the exposure of the first tooth, accounted for these remarkable recoveries. A century later, the ever practical Mrs Boscawen did not wait for further complications when two of her young children became ill, with what she described as tooth fever. The apothecary was called and the gums lanced immediately, with, we are told, satisfactory results.

However, some improvement in the diet of children and babies was to come from an unexpected source in the second half of the eighteenth century. Since their introduction from Peru, in Elizabeth's reign, potatoes had not been cultivated on any scale in England, although they were immediately popular in Ireland. In spite of encouragement from public spirited agriculturists, like John Forster and the Royal Society, the potato continued to be neglected in this country, until a series of disastrous harvests put up the price of bread—the staple diet of the poor. Fear of famine promoted the raising of potatoes on a large scale, helped by the newly formed Board of Agriculture. Irish farmers, with their long experience of cultivating this vegetable, came to England and were soon supplying Covent Garden from market gardens in Ilford and Wanstead.[16] This was so successful that soon potatoes were a routine crop on most arable farms, and the resourceful Governors of the Foundling Hospital made arrangements for their cultivation in the fields that surrounded the Hospital.

For, unlike bread, the potato is a useful source of Vitamin C if taken in sufficient quantities, and the usefulness of the tuber was soon appreciated by its effect on children's health. By 1781, William Moss, a Liverpool surgeon, was advising mothers to avoid bread pap and to give their babies instead a little floury potato mashed in milk, for as he observed, 'this valuable vegetable is one of the great blessings bestowed on this Kingdom, as an article of food'. He readily admitted that the value of the potato was only partially understood, but pointed out that it was especially valuable for children—and what was more, was usually liked by them. By 1840, potatoes had been recognised as a useful cure for scurvy, since their cheapness and availability made them an attractive item of food for poor families.

At the same time, the improvements to the feeding of livestock in winter, with the introduction of turnips and other root vegetables, enabled farmers to overwinter many more of their cattle, and they were no longer obliged to kill and salt down most of their animals each autumn. The availability of fresh meat and potatoes all year round made an enormous difference to the health of the nation, particularly to the children, who were always most vulnerable to the effects of an inadequate diet. During the last twenty-five years of the eighteenth century, the infant mortality figures showed a steady decline, and this improvement persisted into the nineteenth century, although even in 1831, it was estimated that half of the children that were born, in some parts of the country, would die before they were five years old, and the majority of these were under two at the time of their deaths.[17] The introduction of preserved milks in the 1840s, although a great improvement in terms of cleanliness, was a disaster on the vitamin front, and since they quickly became a popular form of infant feeding, there was a rise in the incidence of scurvy and rickets as a result.

Some clues to the underlying causes of these two diseases came in the middle of the nineteenth century, when all attempts to raise bear and lion cubs at the London Zoo, on a diet of lean meat, failed. When cod liver oil, crushed bone, and fresh milk were added, the animals survived, to become the first successfully reared in captivity. Such evidence supported the hypothesis that something more than pure protein, fat and carbohydrate was needed for survival and growth.[18] Further confirmation of the importance of diet in the treatment of scurvy and rickets, came, when Dr Harriette Chick was sent by the Medical Research Council to Vienna in 1919. With the help of cod liver oil and lemon juice, rich sources of the two vitamins, she was able to prevent the appearance of these diseases in children suffering the effects of wartime malnutrition, and to reverse the symptoms when they had already occurred. As a result of her mission, the cause of scurvy and rickets was finally proved to be due to a vitamin deficiency, and not to infection, as many had previously supposed.

During the Second World War, vitamin supplements were made available to all children and nursing mothers. Although there was a general shortage of food, there was no evidence of such vitamin deficiencies, as might have been expected, nor was the period of teething any longer a time of worry and apprehension, as it had been in the past.

For centuries, parents had dreaded the problems associated with teething. From Hippocrates onwards, there had been endless advice as to the best method of weaning, and Dr Cadogan puzzled why some children appeared to have no trouble, while others would die before it was completed. He argued that if, as was generally taught, teething was the cause, then such effects should also be seen with the eruption of the second set of teeth, and this clearly was not so. Until the discovery of the vitamins, there could be no answer to these questions. Undoubtedly, the early curtailing of full breast feeding, by the introduction of pap, would have contributed to the hazards of weaning, and medical disapproval of fresh fruit would have made the provision of a balanced diet even more unlikely. This prejudice against fruit only disappeared when the bacterial cause of diarrhoea was finally recognised in the late nineteenth century. Sadly, it seems possible that those parents who adhered most strictly to medical advice before this, were actually increasing their chances of failure. And it seems ironic that, while in England the doctors were powerless to prevent rickets in the Prince of Wales, across the Irish Sea, the peasants were noted for their health and strength, due mainly, through necessity, to a diet of skimmed milk and potatoes!

6

All Wrapped Up

Swaddling must have been a time-consuming chore, so at first sight it seems strange that this tradition should have persisted for so long. The more so, since older children's clothes were always changing in design, as they followed their parents' fashions. But the continuing appeal of swaddling, in spite of its many drawbacks, was due to its extreme simplicity. For with swaddling bands, like the *sari*, one size fitted all, and these strips of cloth would easily adapt to the growing baby. Made of linen or wool on a hand loom, the bands were usually about three to six inches wide, and some ten feet in length.[1] They required no special care, apart from frequent washing and drying, and it is interesting that none would appear to have survived to be exhibited in the Museums of Costume or Childhood. The swaddling clothes that have been preserved are usually the intricately worked pieces that formed part of the cap or bib, but the more prosaic linen cloths and bands were so simple and easy to make that, like nappies, they were not treasured by mothers once they had outlived their usefulness.

Of course, the primary reason for swaddling was to keep the baby warm, and no doubt the successive layers of linen or wool would have been quite effective in protecting the child from cold and draughts. But such bands were also thought to prevent deformities developing later, and Mrs Sharpe summed up this thinking when she said that babies were tender twigs, and they would grow in the direction in which they were guided.[2] Fear that the naturally flexed limbs of the newborn infant might become a permanent disability made mothers and nurses strive to straighten them as soon as possible after birth, and hold them in this position with the help of such strapping. And following a similar line of argument, it seemed only prudent to hold the head in the upright position as well, until the time when the baby's neck muscles were strong enough to do so unaided. Opponents of such practices pointed out that neither the Scots nor the Irish bound their babies in this way, yet they were noted for their sturdy and straight-limbed children.[3] But while no doubt many parents were aware of these and similar objections to swaddling, when it came to the point, they would have found it difficult to fly in the face of tradition, and run the risk of crippling their own baby for life.

Swaddling must have taken up a considerable amount of the nurse's time. And certainly it was not done without a good deal of preparation—at least in the wealthier home. The windows were tightly shut, and a fire lit in the grate. In many cases the nurse would have a special chair, made of cane. With its seat resting directly on the floor, it looked rather like an elongated dog basket. She would sit as close to the fire as possible with legs outstretched, while the baby lay facing her, supported by a cushion, on her lap.

The child was first cleaned with wine or warm water, and a little capon grease or vegetable oil was rubbed on its bottom to prevent a nappy rash. Linen cloths, called tail clouts, were placed over the buttocks, and then the baby was dressed in an open-fronted vest or jacket. A folded piece of linen called a 'bed' encased the trunk and legs, and Mrs Sharpe reminded her readers at this point that it was important to pull this cloth up between the legs to prevent chafing. Having arranged the infant in its vest and 'bed', the business of swaddling now began.

Rolls of cloth were wound first round the waist, and then diagonally down towards the feet and back again. Similar bands encircled the chest, and when the baby's arms had been placed straight down by its side, these were in turn bound to the already swaddled trunk. A cotton cap, with a pad to protect the fontanelle, was placed on the head, and two further caps put on top of this for greater warmth. To the top of this outermost cap, a strip of linen called a stayband was attached, and when the two ends were pinned to the front of the swaddled chest, it effectively prevented the infant from moving its head from side to side. A cushion, or small mattress, was laid under the child at this stage, and this in turn secured with still more binding to its body. This solid unbending package, which had started out as a small baby, was now almost ready. Although, even then, it was not thought to be completely dressed until it had been covered with a blanket— regardless of the season. By the time the nurse had completed her task, only the child's face was exposed to the air—and even this was commonly covered with a veil, when it lay asleep in its cradle or was taken out of doors.

These babies must have been very hot in summer, and John Evelyn believed that his young son had died from the effects of such overheating, after his nurses had kept him cooped up in a room with sealed windows and close to a blazing fire.[4] This danger was recognised by Dr Buchan, and he recounted how, when he was called to a sick baby, he had been shocked to find it weighed down with clothes. In some instances, such clothing was heavier than the child itself. But in spite of his advice to dress the child more sensibly, on subsequent visits he found it still hopelessly overdressed, and as he had grimly predicted, the child soon died as a result of this treatment.[5]

In unheated houses, the nurse's anxiety to keep her charge warm was understandable, but in some cases this overdressing had an ulterior motive. For although parents were generally advised that their baby should have a complete change of linen, three or four times a day, it seems unlikely that this would have been frequent enough for the healthy baby. And one of the commonest charges brought against hired nurses was that they were too lazy to change the child when it became necessary, and liked to conceal their neglect by covering it up with still more clothes. For since there were no waterproof nappies available, when the baby was wet, it was not long before all the clothing was soaked, and the soiled nappy became a 'permanent poultice'. As all of this was tightly bound to the poor child's skin, it was not surprising that the incidence of skin rashes was high. For even the most careful nurse would have found it difficult to keep up with the many changes that were necessary to keep the baby dry and comfortable.

The earliest nappies were made of smooth cotton or linen, rather like old-fashioned guest towels, and would have been just as useless when it came to absorbing a large volume of fluid.

Probably one of the earliest examples of this type of nappy is worn by the wax effigy of Don Santiago de la Haza y Laguna, which dates from the early eighteenth century.[6] If this doll is anything to go by then English babies must have been not only wet but often very uncomfortable. For the rectangular strip of cloth is wrapped round the baby's loins and buttocks, and fastened between the legs with a large pin. The traditional towelling nappy did not arrive until Victorian times. This marvellous fabric, with loops of cotton on both surfaces, would have been much more absorbent. But when it was washed frequently in hard water it tended to become stiff, and chafed the baby's skin. So by the turn of the century, soft muslin squares were advised as liners for these towelling nappies, and the layette lists of the period make daunting reading with their demands for several dozen of each type. But even these had only a limited absorbency, and the only available remedy was a thick piece of flannel called a pilch or saver, which was placed over the nappy at night and helped to keep the rest of the baby's clothing dry, until it was changed again first thing in the morning.

Although the arrival of the mackintosh in the early nineteenth century was a great bonus for the nursery, it was only thought suitable for covering a baby's mattress.[7] The suggestion that such material could be made into a nappy cover was inevitably condemned on the grounds that it would encourage nursemaids to neglect their charges still further. Later on, oiled silk pilches found favour with writers on childcare, but the suspicion that such aids would only foster laziness persisted, and was still in evidence in the 1950s when most maternity hospitals refused to allow plastic pants to be worn by babies during their stay in hospital—even though the majority of mothers guiltily resorted to them in desperation, as soon as they got home.

Providing that the baby did not need changing, John Pechey reckoned that the commonest reason for its distress arose from tight swaddling or a misplaced pin.[8] But although the constriction from binding that was tighter than usual might have provoked a noisy protest on occasions, the swaddled baby was more often noted for its quiet and undemanding behaviour, since even the full expansion of its chest and lungs was limited by the bands.

However, pins often gave rise to tears when their unguarded

points accidentally pierced the child's skin, for the Danish Safety Pin was not invented until 1878.[9] Up to that time ordinary dressmaker pins were used to fasten the baby's clothing, and since eight to twelve of these were needed for the task, such incidents were commonplace. Richard Steele described how as a baby his clumsy nurse secured his clothes by such means, and when they stuck into him, he began to cry. At which point the girl comforted him with much heavy handed patting, which only drove the nails still further into his flesh and provoked more screams.[10]

Pins were an important item of dress in children and adults alike until only a century or so ago, and when Princess Joanna, the daughter of Edward III, set out for Spain her trousseau included 12,000 pins—surely a lifetime's supply?[11] The numbers that were used in adult clothing were considerable, and when some of these fell to the ground they were retrieved by the sharp-eyed, and resold for 'pin money'. But by Victorian times, wise parents would see that as much of their baby's dress as possible was held together by tapes, and some resorted to sewing their child into its clothes. Even then, one of the essential items of any baby's layette was a large pincushion—which was often embossed with pins that spelt out a message of welcome to the new arrival.

After some weeks, when the baby could hold up its head without help, the rigid stayband was done away with, and the arms were also released from their binding. At this stage, wealthier parents would pin a small pair of sleeves to the child's bodice, and attach an elaborate headdress to the cap. Such additions are seen in the portrait of the two month old Cornelia Burch, even though the lower half of her body remains as tightly swaddled as ever.

The period of swaddling seems to have varied. According to Soranus, the Romans released their babies altogether at six weeks of age, but by the seventeenth century medical writers were advising parents to continue for nine months or more. This probably reflected the increasing incidence of rickets in city children, since it was vainly hoped that a longer period of swaddling might prevent the characteristic bowing of the bones that was seen in this condition.

Whether such advice was ever more than a counsel of perfection is questionable, for it is difficult to believe that the healthy baby would have tolerated such restrictions for so long, and the work that was involved would have been considerable as the child grew older. Although St Bernardino had suggested to mothers that their older daughter should help by washing the swaddling bands, such prolonged swaddling would probably have required the services of a full-time nurse. Certainly, contemporary evidence suggests that country women followed the older practice, and stopped swaddling at six weeks. Both Mary Verney and Charlotte de Tremoille, the Countess of Derby, complained of being badgered by their babies' wet nurses when they did not send on some dresses and petticoats after this time.[12] And this shorter period of swaddling was something that the rest of Europe regarded as particularly English, whatever the medical writers may have advised. Madame de Maintenon wrote in glowing terms of her admiration for this more liberal approach, compared with that of France. In 1707, she noted that 'when they are two or three months old, they are no longer tightly swaddled—but under their dress they wear a wrapper and a loose nappy which is changed as soon as they are soiled—so that the infants never remain, as ours do, tightly swaddled in their own mess'.[13]

But the release from swaddling clothes, whenever it came, did not restore complete liberty to the baby. Although the details varied, the child was usually dressed after this in a shift or petticoat, with a gown over the top. But many nurses still insisted that a broad band or binder should be worn around the trunk, and a pair of stays was *de rigeur*. Boys no longer wore these after they were breeched, but girl babies were condemned to wear some sort of corset for the rest of their lives. When Lady Bryan wrote to complain to Cromwell that her charge, the three year old Princess Elizabeth, had no suitable clothes, stays were high on her list of essential requirements,[14] and it was not until the 1830s that corsets ceased to be a necessary part of a child's wardrobe.

While the baby lay in its cradle, the gown and petticoats covered its feet and helped to keep it warm, but when it began to stand, these would be shortened to prevent it tripping over, and this event was called 'short coating'. Little girls would find their baby's bib replaced by a pinafore, an apron that derived its name from the practice of pinning it to the front of the gown. And both sexes were likely to have a large handkerchief, the aptly named

Muckinder, tied to their belt so that they could be quickly wiped down when they got dirty.

Even though the child had graduated to a gown and petticoats, it was thought essential that it should continue to wear a cap, at least until all the milk teeth had erupted, and night caps were worn for longer. But by the nineteenth century medical opinion was emphasising the importance of keeping the baby's brain cool, and after this time it was no longer customary for caps to be worn indoors. Dr Stockmar actually forbade the wearing of caps and veils in the Royal Nursery,[15] although the practice of covering the baby's face with a veil persisted for much longer. Professor Haldane recalled that, as a small boy in the 1890s, he had protested to nursemaids that he met in the Park when he could not see the faces of the babies that they carried in their arms.[16] In some parts such habits were slow to die out, and it is significant that as late as the 1920s the Mothercraft Manual felt obliged sternly to remind its readers that veils should have no part in the modern baby's layette!

The second half of the eighteenth century saw some of the most important changes in children's dress, which became much less restrictive, while formal swaddling was abandoned for ever. Of course, there had been moves to do this before. As early as 1563, Felix Wurtz had recorded his strong disapproval of swaddling, and suggested that parents should substitute a loose gown with a hood attached, in its place.[17] A century later, John Locke was to express similar views about swaddling, and went on to condemn the overdressing of children in general, on the grounds that it led to spoiling and mollycoddling. He went so far as to suggest that they should be given leaky shoes to wear, so that their feet would always be cold and damp.[18] A batchelor himself, with little experience of small babies, he seemed genuinely suprised when parents did not take to his ideas with greater enthusiasm.

But although swaddling had been criticised for some time, it was the publication of Jean Jacques Rousseau's Emile in 1762 that had a dramatic effect on public opinion. He pointed out that after the comparative freedom of the womb, the baby was no sooner born than it was robbed of its liberty by such swaddling bands. The influence of this book was widespread, and the traditional arguments in favour of swaddling were reappraised. Dr Cadogan had asked his readers in 1748 if it was really likely that 'exact nature' would ever produce an unfinished child. Was there any real evidence that swaddling prevented deformities? These progressive views appealed to the spirit of the time, and after such debates formal swaddling was largely abandoned. Even so, the tradition of centuries did not disappear completely; most nurses were still convinced that some sort of support was necessary for the back and abdomen, and such body binders were to be found in babies' layettes, even at the end of the nineteenth century.

Older children were also to benefit from this new found freedom. They were no longer obliged to wear the formal unbending fashions of their elders, but rather very simple gowns, often made of muslin or cotton, with no more than one petticoat underneath, and fastened at the waist by a sash. These styles are seen in paintings of children after the 1770s, and are often set in rural surroundings. How much the influence Rousseau and Dr Cadogan had on these changes, and how much they reflected the newly aroused love of nature and the countryside, is difficult to determine. But the charm of these clothes may well have had an effect on adult fashion in the Regency period which followed. Sadly, when these grown up styles became more elaborate again, those of young children followed suit, and the Victorian child was as overdressed as its predecessor a hundred years earlier.

Alongside these changes in the design of babies' clothes, others were taking place in the type of fabric of which they were made. Traditionally, linen and later cotton had been favoured by mothers because they could easily be washed and dried. Wool was usually reserved for the outer garments that did not need to be washed so often, but by the second half of the nineteenth century, new manufacturing processes allowed woollen thread to be laundered frequently. Parents were then advised that their infants should always wear white knitted vests next to the skin, and Dr Gustav Jaegar's Sanitary Woollen Wear which was introduced in the 1880s became very popular. Later, wool and cotton were combined in a fabric that had all the advantages of both materials, with few of the drawbacks, and as 'Viyella' was to find a ready market in children's clothing.

In the past twenty years there has been another revolution in babies' dress. Layettes no longer consist of endless bootees and matinee jackets since the arrival of the stretch suit, which followed the development of stretch yarns in North America in the 1960s. This all in one garment will keep the baby warm, even to its hands and feet, yet allows complete freedom of movement. Synthetics have made for easier washdays, while disposable nappies have dispensed with the need for elder daughters to act as laundry maids, as St Bernardino suggested. Even so, midwives and nurses will still hand a child firmly wrapped like a cocoon to its mother, with the comment that a baby so long in the womb likes to feel secure and restricted. And maybe it was the comfort of having a compact firm bundle in the arms, rather than a struggling baby, that helped to keep the custom of swaddling alive for so long.

7

Minding the Baby

Who should mind the baby? For the vast majority of infants in the past, this was the mother's responsibility, helped out no doubt by older relatives, who had time to spare, and older brothers and sisters. Wealthy parents, of course, could afford servants to undertake the task of childminding—while paradoxically very poor mothers would also pay for their children to be minded, in this case because they could not afford the financial luxury of staying at home to do it for themselves. And finally, there was a sad group of orphans and illegitimate children who had no families to look after them. These were dependent on the Parish for their care.

That the mother was seen as the traditional child minder is borne out by the seventh-century *Penitential* of Archbishop Theodore.[1] He stated that if a mother left her swaddled baby by the hearth and it was accidentally scalded by her husband, then the mother must do penance for her negligence—but the child's father was blameless in the matter. Leaving the swaddled baby in front of the fire, or even behind a hot stove, to keep warm, seems to have been common practice, and unable to move in its mummifying bands, the small baby would easily have become overheated if the mother was not very careful. Lying on the floor, the poor infant also ran the risk of being bitten or kicked by any of the animals that were part of the medieval domestic scene, and several writers warned of the dangers of leaving small babies alone for too long.[2] Perhaps it was to avoid these hazards on the ground that the practice arose of hanging the neatly swaddled baby on the wall. A habit that was roundly condemned by Dr Cadogan, describing how 'at the least

14 *Top:* 'The Cobham Family' attributed to Hans Eworth.
This painting also reflects the infant mortality of the time. Of the three
sons in this family portrait, it was the youngest who succeeded to his
father's title.

15 *Bottom:* Cornelia Burch aged two months, 1581.
In her right hand she holds a combined rattle and teething stick.

16 *Top:* 'The Cholmondeley Sisters', c. 1600.
The inscription reads that they were born the same day, married the same day, and brought to Bed the same day.

17 *Bottom:* 'The Adoration of the Shepherds' by Georges de la Tour.
A 17th-century painting of a swaddled baby.

18 *Top:* 'La Visite à la Nourrice' by Abraham Bosse.
While the wet nurse attends to the baby, its mother rewinds a
swaddling band, and a maidservant airs the baby's clothing in front of
the fire.

19 *Bottom:* 'Farewell to the Nurse' by Etienne Aubry.
The concern shown by the wet nurse and her husband for the child who
is leaving them is in sharp contrast to the stance of the natural father
who is waiting to start the journey home.

20 'Nurse with Child' by Frans Hals.
The richness of the baby's clothes suggests that the family must have
been very wealthy, while the striking resemblance between the two
would support the traditional view that such children grew to look like
their nurses.

21 *Top:* 'The Blunt Children'
by Zoffany.
The simplicity of the Blunt
children's dresses in the last
quarter of the 18th century
contrasts with that of four-
year-old Princess Victoria in
the 1820s.

22 *Right:* 'Princess Victoria'
by Stephen Poyntz-Denning.

23 *Top:* 'The Flight into Egypt' by Giotto.
The infant Jesus is held close to his mother by a sling.

24 *Bottom left:* Two medieval solutions to the problem of carrying small children.

25 *Bottom right:* Wayfarers from the 14th century.
Medieval travellers. The swaddled infant is carried in the arms, while the older, and heavier, child is carried on the back in a makeshift papoose.

26 *Top left:* The Duchess of Gosse.
The Duchess of Gosse with her daughter in a wicker cradle on wheels in the 18th century.

27 *Top right:* A portrait of the artist's wife and child in Windsor Park by Paul Sandby, RA.

28 *Bottom:* The children of James I.
Prince Henry wears a small sword, but is still young enough at the age of five years to be dressed in skirts. The two-year-old Prince Charles is probably still teething as he wears a cap and has a teething stick hanging from a ribbon round his neck. It would seem that there was no objection to boys playing with dolls in the 17th century. His sister, Princess Elizabeth, aged four years, holds his leading string. A well upholstered baby walker is in the foreground.

29 *Top:* Queen Victoria with her young family in Windsor Park. Note the length of the baby Prince's gown.

30 *Bottom:* Father pulls the Stick Wagon, from a magazine of 1833.

annoyance which arises he is hung from a nail like a bundle of old clothes, and while without hurrying the nurse attends to her business, the unfortunate one remains thus crucified'. Seeing such a child with a purple face and scarcely able to breathe, he warned the mother that she should not be surprised if this sort of baby-minding eventually led to the death of her precious infant.

Of course, the young baby had no choice but to stay still while it was kept in swaddling bands, but when these were discarded and it became more mobile, it would require a good deal more care if it was not to injure itself. The writer of the *Regimen for Young Children* in the fifteenth century, advised parents to construct a little pen of leather when the baby began to crawl.[3] About the same time other writers showed designs for an infant's chair, with a bar across the arms to prevent the baby escaping, and some of these even had a potty in the seat for good measure. For the child was expected to spend several hours at a time in such a contraption, and to make sure that it did not get cold, a small heater filled with charcoal was sometimes put in the base.

As a further modification, a little tray was often attached to the restraining bar, and the baby's food and toys would be placed on it. The illustration shows a toddler for whom these usual diversions have long ago lost their charm and already a doll and spoon have hit the floor, while the child attempts to attract its mother's attention by the well worn ruse of getting her to pick them up again. The history of children's toys is an enormous subject, but it is interesting that the baby's first toys have remained very similar in concept over the years. Such pictures of small children often contain rattles and teething sticks that would have made an entertaining noise when they were banged on their tray, while small balls and dolls were equally common. But even at this early age, keen parents were also anxious to use toys to educate their baby. ABC blocks were introduced in Elizabeth's reign and a small rocking horse was used to teach Charles I the rudiments of riding, before he was allowed to try the real animal.

But this sort of diversion required the full time attention of the childminder. For the busy mother who did not have the time to spare from her other household duties, the standing stool could be very helpful. A Victorian illustration shows such a stool simply made from a section of hollowed out tree trunk, and rather resembling an umbrella stand. The young baby, often no more than six months old, would be propped up in this cylinder—the diameter of which was small enough to hold him upright. Once inside, the baby could not move, not even to bend his knees, and with this reassurance the mother or nurse would get on with her other work. These stools were not new. Felix Wurtz had condemned their use in 1563, when he wrote that he wished that all such stools were burnt, since the child was often left in them for hours on end, whereas in his opinion even half an hour was too much.[4] But like all successful baby minding inventions, the harassed minder was often tempted to use them for far too long, and what started out as a means of entertaining the baby, often developed into a miserable restraint.

However, the walking frame or go-cart seems to have given more pleasure to its users—even though it was also criticised for encouraging neglect. But there is a happier picture of young Thomas, Lord Erskine, running 'up and down the room in an excellent machine made of willows'. Such games were limited though, since his grandmother was anxious that he should not strain his legs for too long and we are told that 'my lady takes care that he does not stress himself with walking too much'.[5] This idea of a frame on wheels that would hold the young baby upright, while it pushed itself around, was obviously a Godsend to all childminders. Illustrations for such frames appeared as early as the fifteenth century, and were popular in nurseries as far apart as Scotland and Italy. There was a thriving export trade of these walkers from London to Edinburgh in the seventeenth century,[6] and turners' shops in Liverpool Street made a speciality of their manufacture.[7] They often appeared in contemporary portraits, and one is seen in the foreground, in a family group of James I's children. It is interesting that the basic design of such go-carts has not changed substantially over the centuries, and the modern baby walker is very similar to that seen in such paintings, although today it is more likely to be made of aluminium and plastic, rather than willow or turned wood.

The baby walker, once described as the 'infantile playground' on wheels,[8] no doubt gave a lot of pleasure and exercise to the toddler—but it required space, a Long Gallery or passage, or at least a fair sized room. For families who lived in cramped conditions, such as weavers, whose looms might almost fill the cottage in which they lived, the problem of both exercising and at the same time, restraining, the baby was solved by another device, the baby walk or gin. The child was placed in a wooden belt, which rotated around a central pole that was fixed vertically between ceiling and floor. Although the toddler could circle around his 'maypole' in either direction, he was safely prevented from leaving his limited exercise area while his parents got on with their work.

The baby's first hesitant steps were often accompanied by falls and to protect his head at this time the toddler wore a sort of crash helmet. Called a Pudding, it consisted of a padded circlet of cloth that went around the child's brow and was tied under the chin by strings. Illustrations show this to have been in use in the sixteenth century, and they continued to be popular in the nursery until the early 1800s, when, according to a contemporary source, they went out of favour for some reason.[9] Leading strings, or reins, were also liked by nurses, since by holding on to these they could prevent the toddler from falling to the ground when it stumbled. In wealthy families these restrainers were often made of the same material as the baby's dress, and incorporated into the design of the bodice, although Catherine Verney demanded specially strong ties for her son, Jak, as he was very heavy for his age. But doctors were less than happy with these reins as they pointed out that the lazy nurse would prefer to drag her charge along by his leading strings when he was tired, rather than carry him in her arms. And they feared that the deformity produced by jerking the child's shoulders upwards in this way, would lead in time to a permanent distortion of the spine.

However, there is no doubt that the harassed mother would have been grateful for some of these aids to childminding, and even more grateful for another's help in watching that her baby came to no harm. But the idea of employing a servant specifically to care for the children does not seem to have occurred until the seventeenth century. Before this, the Lady of the House, with her almost encyclopaedic knowledge of running the household, would expect any of her servants to keep an eye on the children, as one of the many tasks that they carried out each day.

Nan Fudd, who served two generations of the Verney family,

was an example of this newer type of babyminder—the nanny.[10] These children's servants were expected to dress their charges, and teach them to speak clearly and repeat simple prayers. Later they would hear their first lessons. As time went on, they exercised still more influence, as mothers handed over the day to day running of the nursery to them. And after such a nurse had successfully cared for several children, her views and opinions on child raising would have been listened to with respect. No doubt for many families, like the Verneys, the children's nanny was a treasure, but the system was open to abuse, and it is significant that from the seventeenth century onwards, writers, such as Locke and later Rousseau, were always anxious to warn parents not to depend on servants for their child's upbringing, but rather to undertake the task for themselves. Only then could they be sure that their offspring were not led into bad ways. For many servants were scarcely more than children themselves, and they felt little responsibility towards their charges. Such warnings persisted, even into the Victorian era, and mothers were always advised to keep a close eye on the nursery servants, to the extent of making a surprise visit to the park, where the children were taken for exercise.

The Victorian age was to see the heyday of the nanny, for with more children, especially amongst the middle classes, surviving into adult life, large families were commonplace. These children and their attendants needed a suite of rooms to themselves and this was customarily provided at the top of the house. For as servants were both plentiful and cheap, the nanny was often helped by several lesser mortals, who either assisted with the older children or undertook the domestic work of the nursery. The youngest child was always the nanny's special charge, until another baby came along to take its place, and on walks in the park the youngest baby's perambulator was pushed by her, with the assistant nurse-maids helping the older children in the family. Living in their own private kingdom, with so many servants to care for them, this was probably one of the safest periods of childminding, for those who could afford it. With bars on the windows to prevent accidents, a fireguard in front of the grate, and surrounded by a small group of adults who were always on hand to help—no wonder that the Victorian nursery is thought of with nostalgia and affection.

But the nanny, although given the courtesy title of 'Mrs' was, unlike the wet nurse, usually unmarried and rarely a mother herself. She had no training, apart from that acquired in her progression from nursery maid to chief nurse. Such women were a veritable store of knowledge and ignorance which was the mainstay of the nursery. Their influence was immense. Sir Winston Churchill wrote of his own nanny, after her death, 'she had been my dearest and most intimate friend during the whole of the twenty years that I had lived'. A glowing tribute to a remarkable woman—but others were less so—and some were downright tyrants. With age and experience, they would expect to run the nursery with little reference to the parents. And as a mother's childbearing years often extended until her eldest children had married themselves, it was not uncommon for mother and daughter to have children of the same age. Queen Victoria had found herself pregnant with her youngest child, Princess Beatrice, only two years before her eldest daughter gave birth to her first son, the future Kaiser Wilhelm. Under such circumstances, the experienced nanny was often swapped backwards and forwards between generations of a family—establishing the same nursery routine in a daughter's household that she had organised in the parents' home some years earlier.

By the twentieth century, the training of a nanny was put on a more formal basis, with the opening of colleges and training schools where orthodox instruction on childcare and hygiene was taught. Emphasis was also laid on respect for the parents' wishes in matters of upbringing and, by recruiting girls from middle class homes, the colleges transformed the status of the nanny from that of domestic servant to a profession. Modern nannies tend to spend shorter times with their chosen families and to change more often to an entirely different one, but it is still possible for a nanny to stay in one extended family for the whole of her working life. The Queen's nanny, Mabel Anderson, was to pass to other members of the Royal family before returning to nurse Master Peter Phillips, the Queen's first grandchild. And having cared for Princess Anne when she was a baby, she must have approached the task of running her son's nursery with an almost grandmotherly perspective.

But for those parents who could not afford a living-in nurse, the problem of childminding was often solved by sending the baby to the local dame school. Such ladies, often with only a modicum of knowledge themselves, undertook to teach young children their letters and prayers, and certain crafts, such as sewing and spinning, that would be useful to them in later life. At the same time, they were happy to keep an eye on those babies and toddlers who were too young to be taught, so young in fact, that they were carried to school in their mother's arms. It was customary to place a board across the open door, to prevent these very young children from wandering off while the teacher's back was turned, and they were often tied by a cord to her chair—or even pinned by a giant pin to her skirts, as she sat teaching the older pupils.[11] 'Tied to a mother's apron strings' is a saying that has persisted into the twentieth century, but it reflects the childminding practices of a much earlier age.

These dame schools were usually conducted in the teacher's own home, and it is unlikely that any were refused if they could afford the modest fee. Conditions must have been very cramped at times, and any infection would have spread like wildfire from one to another. No wonder that Dr Buchan appealed to parents to keep their young babies at home if they possibly could. For although he admitted that looking after a toddler could be an exhausting business, which put a great strain on the mother, he felt that sending a baby to such a crowded school was no better than sending it to the Pest House. And he urged parents to look for another solution to their childminding problems.

But the problem of minding the baby became more difficult for the very poor family as the eighteenth century progressed. For while cottage industries flourished, the mother could get by with a combination of a few pence spent on minding at the local dame school, and help from older children, who were not yet at work. But the real problem of minding the baby arose when the mother went out to work in the factory. Following the Industrial Revolution, the drift of the poorer population into the new manufacturing towns led to many hardships, not least that of caring for the younger children while the mother went out to work in the factory. These families were so poor that they could only afford the most desperate means of looking after their small children. Each morning they were left with old women who made a living by caring for large numbers of these babies for a pittance, and it was not until late at night that these infants were collected by their tired mothers and taken home again. Disraeli wrote graphically of such a mother and the usual result in his novel *Sybil*.

'About a fortnight after his mother had introduced him into the world, she returned to her factory, and put her infant out to nurse—that is to say, paid threepence a week to an old woman, who takes charge of these new-born babes for the day, and gives them back at night to their mothers, as they hurriedly return from the scene of their labour to the dungeon or den, which is still by courtesy called "home". The expense is not great: laudanum and treacle, administered in the shape of some popular elixir, affords these innocents a brief taste of the sweets of existence, and, keeping them quiet, prepares them for the silence of their impending grave. Infanticide is practised as extensively and as legally in England, as it is on the banks of the Ganges.'

Laudanum, or morphia, was freely available over the counter, in several preparations. One of the most popular was Godfrey's cordial. In 1843, such was the demand for this medicine, which was used solely for children, that one pharmacist made up thirteen hundredweight of treacle into the elixir![12] Not surprisingly, its use as a sedative was often abused—so much so, that in 1776, Dr Hume claimed that thousands of children died each year from the effects of this cordial. And when Dr Buchan was appointed to the Ackworth Foundling Hospital, he discovered that a great deal of opiates had been prescribed for the inmates, perhaps because the apothecaries were paid a dispensing fee for each medicine, and the temptation to overprescribe was strong. When Dr Buchan refused to continue this practice of indiscriminate prescribing, the mortality rate fell dramatically.

If a working family was in better circumstances, then it was often the practice to employ a young girl or old woman to care for the children in her own home, and in return these helpers would be given their meals and perhaps a few pence a week. Dr Buchan had been appalled by the sight of small children wandering the city streets by day, often in the charge of minders who were not much more than eight years old themselves. But in spite of his criticism, this was still a preferable method of childminding, for at least the numbers of children were limited, and the family home, however poor, would have been better than the squalor of the professional babyminder.

Attempts were made in the late nineteenth century to legislate for a certain standard of childminding—taking into account both the quality of the minder, and the surroundings in which the child was kept. Sadly, poor families only saw this proposed legislation as a further burden, since by demanding reasonable standards of care, the cost of minding would inevitably rise. And there was no question of offering parents compensation for their extra expense. As a result, it was not until 1948 that a register was introduced for paid childminders, who looked after a child for more than two hours a day. Such private childminding arrangements were still very much in demand, since the number of places that were available in Day Nurseries was severely limited. By the late 1960s however, some of this need was being satisfied by pre-school playgroups, which were largely founded by self-help organisations. This concept proved a popular one, and very soon flourishing playgroups were being set up in all parts of the country.

However, the State has long been involved, either directly or indirectly, with the care of orphans, or children that were abandoned by their families, in many cases because they were illegitimate. In 1597, Parliament firmly put the responsibility for organising the care of this growing problem with the parish in which the child lived. There had always been a somewhat ambivalent attitude to illegitimacy. On the whole, the wealthy bastard was acceptable to society, and it was only the baby that threatened to be a burden on the parish that was shameful. For in the middle ages, not only did the rich nobleman bring up his natural children alongside his legitimate heirs, but on occasions, the Lady of the Manor was recorded as having done likewise. Such babies, freely acknowledged and supported by their parents, caused few difficulties.

But abandoned or orphaned babies, with no means of support, were always a problem, and depended on charity for their care. The first legislation for assisting the children of the poor was made in 1536, and Christ's Hospital was founded to help some of London's poor and destitute orphans.[13] However, the majority of these children were the responsibility of the parish overseer, and it was his duty to arrange foster care for them, and later to see that they were apprenticed to a suitable trade. But having made these arrangements, the parish was sometimes slow to pay its debts, and there is an instance of such a nurse petitioning the courts for maintenance due for her three foster children. For, as she quite reasonably pointed out, she was a poor woman and already had three children of her own to support.[14]

The problem of these parish children increased during the seventeenth century, when the Civil War led to a fall of revenue to many charitable foundations, and some had to stop caring for children altogether. Yet the war inevitably led to an increase in the numbers of orphans and destitute children. At the same time, parishes were more anxious than ever to keep their expenses to an absolute minimum. It became common practice to give the nurse a lump sum for the care of the baby, and this often amounted to no more than the cost of one year's board. No doubt, rate-payers were delighted to be free of all future responsibility in this way, but it was common knowledge that babies put out to nurses for such single payments seldom survived for long.

This lack of money, coinciding with an actual increase in numbers, led to harsher remedies, and resulted in the concept of the workhouse. In such institutions, children could be kept under spartan conditions and encouraged to earn their keep from an early age. Daniel Defoe saw no reason why children of four or five years of age should not earn enough to defray the cost of their board and lodging, as they did in Norwich.[15] It was not long before the number of parish children that perished, either as a result of being sent to unscrupulous nurses, or being cared for in such grim institutions, became a national scandal. But many were frightened that any improvements would only encourage more parents to abandon their babies. However, in spite of such fears, there was a growing body of opinion in the early eighteenth century that sought the setting up of more humane establishments, on the lines of the foundling homes that were already to be found in some parts of the Continent.

Understandably, desperate mothers would often leave their unwanted babies on the doorsteps of wealthy families, in the hope that they would be taken in out of charity. But many babies were not even privileged to this start in life, and were found abandoned by the roadside, or on rubbish heaps. This was so common by

1719, that Captain Thomas Coram, who had recently returned to England, was horrified to see such infants beside the road, on his frequent journeys from Rotherhithe to London.[16] Childless himself, he began, although already over fifty, to campaign vigorously for a more humane institution, to which such children could be sent. His aim was two-fold, to care for the babies that would otherwise die by neglect, and to give the unmarried mother a fresh start and an opportunity to return to the path of virtue.

For twenty years he built up support for such an establishment, and finally in 1739 he was given a Royal Charter. Two years later, the first of ninety children were admitted to the new Foundling Hospital. So great was the demand for these places, that watchmen were placed outside the building to make sure that no disappointed mother abandoned her baby after it had been refused admission. For the next fifteen years, the hospital continued to accept about ninety babies a year, and so high was its reputation for care, that when in 1756, the Governors applied to Parliament for financial aid, it was given £10,000 on the condition that in future it accepted all the babies under the age of twelve months that were presented to it.

Amazingly, arrangements were swiftly made for the provision of more accommodation. Other Foundling Hospitals were opened in parts of the country where the children were likely to find apprenticeships and employment later in life. In all, over the next four years, 15,000 babies were accepted—sometimes arriving at the hospital at the rate of 200 a week. Many of these infants were in a pathetic state on arrival, and two-thirds of them died within the first month of life, in spite of all efforts to save them. An empty basket was left outside the porter's lodge for the reception of the babies, and some were found completely naked, as their parents could not afford to part with their few clothes, while others were moribund, being left in this state to save their families the cost of burial. Those children who survived, were fed by the resident wet nurses for the first few days, and on the Sunday following admission, were baptised in the hospital chapel, given new names, and later sent to the country, where they stayed with their foster nurse until they were about five years old. After this, they returned to the Foundling Hospital, and were later apprenticed to outside masters. The enormous numbers of children admitted during this four year period led to one embarrassment—they ran out of names, and having been through the usual ones, we are told that they were forced to go to the Zoo for their inspiration!

After four years, this open policy was brought to an end, and the Foundling Hospital reverted to its previous system of admitting about ninety children a year. However, the problem of caring for all the other parish children in London, and for that matter in England, still remained to be solved. Jonas Hanway, a governor of the Foundling Hospital, and a man who was passionately interested in the welfare of poor children, had investigated the records of London parishes, during the years 1750–1755.[17] His findings were appalling. In many, not one child survived after being put out to nurse. Indeed, he was told that in one parish such ladies were known as 'excellent killing nurses'. The indifference of the overseer to everything but the saving of money had helped to perpetuate these systems of abuse. In the parish of St Clement Danes, a Mrs Poole had cared for twenty-three infants, of which eighteen had died within a month or so of coming to her. She had been paid at the rate of two shillings a week, for each baby. In Whitechapel, it was the practice to pay nurses two shillings and sixpence a week—and this extra sixpence seems to have made all the difference, for Mrs Howe, who had been sent eighteen infants at that rate, had only lost two during the same period.[18]

Public opinion was shocked by Hanway's revelations. His solution was simple. In future, all London parishes should publicly declare the number of children that they were supporting. The comparison of such scandalous mortality rates with those of better parishes would force parsimonious parish officers to improve their systems of relief. Very soon a law was introduced that obliged these parishes to register all the children under four years that they were supporting. The penalty to the churchwarden who failed to do this was a fine of forty shillings, made payable—a nice touch this—to the informer!

Hanway himself said that the common people called this act of 1762, 'the act for keeping poor children alive', and he reckoned that 500 babies would be saved annually in London as a result. As he had hoped, when the parishes did set about improving their care for destitute children, they turned to the Foundling Hospital for practical guidance. And when in 1763, St James, Westminster reorganised itself, it was decided to send all their parish babies to cottagers on Wimbledon Common, at the rate of three shillings a week. Each nurse was to receive no more than five or six children at a time, and a local physician was to be engaged to care for their health. A small bonus would be paid to the nurse when the child reached one year of age, and at other milestones in its life. Should the infant be successfully nursed through a severe illness, she would be given a further reward, and a similar payment would be made to herself and the doctor if the baby was inoculated against smallpox. However, should more than two children die while in her care, then she would no longer be eligible to foster further babies.

When one compares this attitude with the system that Hanway had found in even the best parishes in 1755, it is not suprising that there was such a discrepancy in infant mortality rates between them. In later years, many parishes were to incorporate similar ideas into their own regulations, with consequent success. And by 1768, Hanway had managed to ensure that no London parish would keep a baby for more than two weeks in its workhouse, without making arrangements for the child to be sent to a nurse, who must live at least five miles outside the great metropolis.[19] But although there were many improvements as a result of his legislation, there was always the difficulty of enforcing the law, when the problem was so widespread.

Hanway's legislation, although revolutionary, had only applied to the London parishes. For the great majority however, the workhouse was to remain the usual method of caring for the destitute child, and by the nineteenth century most of their young inmates were illegitimate. Orphanages founded by private charities often refused to admit such babies—fearing that the moral tone of their establishments would be lowered if they did. But there was one notable exception. Today, the name of Dr Barnardo is inextricably linked with the image of the Victorian orphanage, but he always refused to make any moral judgement about a baby's origins, and proudly proclaimed that *no* destitute child was ever refused admission to his homes.[20] As a young medical student, he had seen at first hand the desperate plight of homeless children in Whitechapel. On bitterly cold nights, hordes of these half-starved urchins were forced to sleep rough, and many finally died of exposure. Initially, he set about providing food and shelter for such children, and later attempted to replace some of the family life that they had lost, by building houses for groups of children, of varying ages, under the supervision of a house mother. These homes, spartan and grim to modern eyes, were nevertheless founded on noble ideals and revolutionary in their concept at the time.

But since that time, the pendulum has swung far in the opposite direction, and during recent years the number of orphaned children available for adoption has dropped dramatically. Today, an abandoned baby usually makes the national newspapers, such is its rarity value, closely followed by an overwhelming demand by would-be parents to care for it. But although it is sad to think of their inevitable disappointment, it is infinitely better than the prospect of unwanted babies on the road to Rotherhithe, that Captain Coram saw in the eighteenth century.

But at the same time changes have also occurred in the home in the last seventy years. For a social revolution has done away with servants for all but the very rich, and as far as childminding is concerned, today's mother has probably more in common with her Elizabethan counterpart than with her own grandmother. That same revolution, of course, has made the working mother unexceptional at all levels of society, so that the problem of who is to mind the baby is a common one.

Perhaps the ideal arrangement, if circumstances permit, is for the parents to share the task between them, although in practice it is far more likely that a grandparent or other relative will do the minding if they live nearby. If this is not possible, then some mothers organise a sort of barter system, minding a neighbour's child at times so that they can have free babysitting in return.

But if a mother plans to return to full-time work shortly after her baby is born, then she will need to make very definite arrangements. The traditional nanny, who shared the family home for years, is a rare bird these days, and today's children's nurse often prefers to work the office hours of her employers. This solution works suprisingly well in practice, for many parents are delighted to enjoy the privacy of their family when they return home, even if it involves them in extra work. And in some cases they may decide to offset the cost of employing such a highly trained minder during the day, by sharing her with another family in similar circumstances.

But a nanny is not the only solution to the problem of child-minding for the working mother. Mother's helps, although they have no professional training, often have considerable experience of caring for small children. And if the mother only plans to be out of the home for a few hours each day, then an *au pair*, who lives in with the family for six to twelve months, may prove to be an excellent deputy. If it is not feasible for the baby to be cared for in the familiar environment of its own home, then a suitable child-minder or day nursery is the most likely solution. Sadly, the work *crèche*, although fairly common on the Continent, is rare in this country and those that do exist are nearly always oversubscribed.

Today, the variety of childminding options that are available to the working mother are much the same as they have always been, with one important exception. For in recent years, the baby's father has become involved in caring for his children in a way that would have been almost unthinkable to earlier generations. But whoever is responsible for minding the child, the continuing demand for playpens and baby walkers suggests that it is still no easy task to keep an energetic and adventurous toddler out of harm's way.

8

Moving Around

However convenient swaddling may have been for the mother or nurse, for the baby held fast in its bands, the lack of any natural exercise was an enormous drawback. This worried parents, because it was suspected that such immobility might lead to rickets. So nurses were told to bounce the baby up and down a good deal during the course of the day, in the naive belief that such passive movement would be a good substitute for the child's natural activity. And as early as 1612, Jacques Guillemeau was advising parents that after the first three weeks or so of life, part of this exercise should be taken out of doors. Considering the dangers that were thought to be lurking in the outside air, it seems rather surprising that the nurse should have been encouraged to take her charge out of doors like this. And it is interesting that the prevention of rickets was already associated with fresh air and exercise—three centuries before the nature of the 'sunshine vitamin' was known.

Dancing the baby up and down in her arms for long periods would have required a great deal of stamina, and Sir Roger Newdigate advised his daughter to find a nurse that was both stout and nimble enough to cope with the tumbling and tossing that his small grandson required all day long.[1] And perhaps it was to relieve the tedium that in some families such exercises developed into horseplay, and the solid swaddled package was thrown from one to another, rather like a rugby ball! Inevitably there were accidents, and something of this sort seems to have happened to the baby brother of the future French King, Henri IV, when he was accidentally dropped from an upstairs window, and died as a result of his injuries.[2]

Fortunately, such fatal incidents seem to have been rare, but wealthy families often employed a couple of young girls to take over this task of entertaining and exercising the baby all day long, which, no doubt, would have come as a great relief to the nurse. Rockers, as these young servants were called, were expected to carry the infant around in their arms while soothing it with lullabies, or if the child was in a more lively mood, to jog it up and down on their knees to old nursery rhymes like 'Dancy Baby Diddy'. Even when the baby was laid in its cradle at night, it was possible to continue this all important programme of infantile gymnastics, and the nurse, having first made sure that her charge was safely strapped in, would rock it to sleep. But if the baby showed no sign of sleeping, then ignorant nursemaids often rocked the cradle so violently that the child's brain was numbed by the motion. According to Dr Buchan, this sort of thing was commonplace, and he deplored the necessity for such passive exercise, which would not have been needed if swaddling had been abandoned altogether, as he had long advised.

But when the child was freed from its bands, and began to show signs of wanting to crawl, there was no uniformity of opinion about the benefits. Mauriceau had condemned it outright, as animal-like, and feared that if the baby was allowed to crawl such bestial behaviour might persist into adult life. On the other hand, all the evidence from the New World supported the opposite view, and John Locke noted that the inhabitants of the Gold Coast placed no such restrictions on their babies, so that they scrambled around on all fours, like kittens. As a result, they actually learnt to walk earlier than their western counterparts, and, most important of all, they showed no signs of weakness later.

For there had always been concern about the best time for the child to attempt to stand. This worry probably reflected the high incidence of rickets in infancy, since the bowing of the legs, which was so characteristic of the disease, was usually noticed for the first time when the child stood upright. Understandably, it was concluded that the weight of the baby's body had been too much for its young limbs, which had buckled under the strain. And when Chancellor Audley reported to Henry VIII on the health of his son, the eleven month old Prince Edward, in 1538, he assured the King that his heir was fit and now able to stand. But he was careful to add that he had no doubt that the young prince could also walk, were it not that his nurses were resolved to restrain him 'lest his legs be injured'.[3]

Soranus had written about the problem of bandy children in the first century, and according to him, they were a common sight in Rome at that time. He had warned parents that both premature sitting and standing was the likely cause, and this teaching seems to have been accepted without much further argument, by later generations of physicians. That is, until the eighteenth century, when Dr Buchan not only disputed the theory, but actually dared to suggest that early standing and walking, far from leading to weakness, would actively strengthen the child's bones. Even so, the notion persisted that a baby could be too heavy for its legs to support, and as late as 1924, an American paediatrician was still warning parents that premature walking might lead to bandy legs.[4] And it is fascinating that although the cause of rickets is now known, traces of this old idea linger on, and doctors are still asked, on occasion, whether a child is old enough to stand.

But long before the baby's walking became a problem, it needed to travel. The first journey was invariably to church for its baptism, which in medieval times was usually within the first three days of birth. And carried the short distance to the parish church in its godmother's arms, the newborn baby was unlikely to have been much of a burden. A rather more unusual procession was recorded in 1575, by John Stow—when one month after their birth, quadruplets were the chief mourners at their own mother's funeral—and were carried behind the coffin into the church.[5]

However, when the baby was sent away to nurse, it was sometimes carried twenty miles or more, and the effort of carrying the two-week old Charles Framlingham from his home at Shelley Hall, to Crowshall, near Debenham, was not something that his nurse would have forgotten in a hurry. She was able to recall this arduous journey many years later, when as an old woman of seventy-two years, in Elizabeth's reign, she testified to the date of the boy's birth—adding significantly that it was a long hot summer that year.[6] Carrying bigger children on journeys would have been even more onerous, and an illustration of medieval

travellers, said to be members of Thomas à Becket's family fleeing
to France, shows a small swaddled baby being carried in the arms,
but the older child, who would have been too heavy to be held
in this way, is slung in a makeshift papoose on the traveller's
back.

When Mary Verney decided to send her newborn son to
Claydon, in the seventeenth century, she gave detailed instruc-
tions to her steward. The wet nurse was clearly anxious to get
home to her own family, and assured her mistress that her
husband had a very gentle horse that would manage the journey
without trouble. Even then, Mary Verney was at pains to point out
to the Steward that if the man carried the baby in front of him on a
cushion, he should make certain that he was tied to him by a
garter.[7] A similar idea is seen in Giotto's painting of the journey
into Egypt, and it is not unlike the baby slings that have become
very popular in recent years. Mothers seem to like these carriers
because they can hold their babies close to them, while they move
around, and Mary Verney probably liked the sling for the same
reason, for she wrote that the baby would not long endure to be
out of her arms.

Royalty usually made more elaborate arrangements before a
journey, as in 1306, when Edward I's five week old daughter,
Eleanor, had to travel from Winchester to the royal nursery in
Northampton. Progress must have been very slow, for she took
sixteen days to arrive at her destination. Unaccompanied by her
parents—although she must presumably have travelled with her
nurse, she lay in her cradle, which was carried inside a litter that
was covered in green cloth and lined with crimson silk. The litter
was carried by two men on horseback, who wore a new blue livery
for the occasion. Sadly, no member of her family was present
either, when she died five years later, and made her final lonely
journey to be buried in great state at Beaulieu.[8]

Poorer families were often compelled to take their children with
them when they worked in the fields, and Wyclif mentioned that
small carts, or 'waynes', were used to transport those infants, who
were perhaps too young to walk as far as their parents, but too
heavy to be carried for any distance. A medieval manuscript shows
other solutions to the problem for younger babies, a peasant
carries two swaddled babies, toe to toe, in an ingenious canoe-

shaped basket, while another has two more infants in a pannier on his back. [Fig. 3]

And as the nursery rhyme suggests, mothers often hung their baby's cradle from the branch of a tree, while they worked out of doors, and allowed the breeze to play rocker, as it gently lulled the child into contentment. These children would have been out in the fresh air for most of the day in fine weather, and perhaps it was because of such country children's reputed good health that Jacques Guillemeau advised that part of the swaddled baby's day should be spent out of doors in its nurse's arms. That was always providing, of course, that she lived in a healthy part of the country, for Mrs Sharpe warned parents never to entrust their child to a woman who lived near a bog, or close to the sea. In seventeenth-century England, marshy land was still a likely breeding ground for mosquitoes, and the pattern of fever seen in malaria was well known, so such advice is understandable. Disapproval of the seaside seems at first sight to be rather odd, but it may have originated from a fear of salt, that was thought to be a cause of scurvy.

But in spite of these worries, as time went on, there was a growing appreciation of the value of fresh air for children, and when Mrs Boscawen rented a house for the summer near Windsor she deliberately chose one which, in her words, had a lawn for her children to play on when it was cool, and a wood that they could shelter in when it became too hot.[9] Even when in London, she made sure that they went to Hyde Park each day from their Audley Street home. Nor did fear of early morning chills and dampness prevent her from taking her small son into the garden before breakfast, until his shoes were wet with dew, for she observed that he never seemed to catch cold after such adventures. Of course, she was remarkably open-minded in her approach to childcare, but by the late eighteenth century, most doctors were endorsing the child's need for regular outdoor exercise. Far from being dangerous to the baby, it was positively beneficial for its health and development, and if the mother joined her child on these excursions, she would not only keep an eye on the nurse-maids—but improve her own health at the same time.

Perhaps it was in response to this new approach that as time went on, more and more pleasure gardens and parks opened up for city dwellers. Families were able to enjoy the facilities of places like Vauxhall and the Adam and Eve gardens, in Tottenham Court Road. But to get there, young babies still had to be carried in the arms. It seems strange that it took another century before the perambulator became popular for young infants in England, particularly as the Duchess of Gosse had such a mobile cradle on wheels in mid-eighteenth-century France [Fig. 4], and the idea of a miniature carriage for older children was not new. The future Queen Anne had a small carriage for her young son, Prince William of Gloucester. It was a christening gift from the Duchess of Ormond, and was drawn by two shetland ponies. A local boy, Dick Drury, acted as coachman, and every morning the little carriage was driven backwards and forwards on the path beneath the Princess's window. This exercise was thought to be so important that his parents even allowed the young Prince to miss family devotions on this account, if the weather was fine.[10]

A similar carriage, dating from the 1730s, can be seen at Chatsworth. It was made for the children of the Third Duke of Devonshire, and beside it there is a later model that was designed with only one shaft, that could be pulled by a manservant, rather than a small pony. These man-powered carriages seem to have become very popular amongst the well-to-do, who could afford to commission such a vehicle from their coach builders. They often appeared in family portraits—but it is significant that they are either shown with a footman in attendance, or else the older children are making play of doing the moving. For the task of pulling such a carriage by its central pole would have been both clumsy and difficult, and would not have been contemplated by people of quality! And although less affluent families had small chairs on wheels, they were pulled in the same way. The illustration of a mother beside such a chair suggests that a journey of any distance would still have been a considerable chore.

When there were several small children in the family, little carts were used, called stick wagons. They were probably modelled on the hop carts that day labourers used for transporting both their progeny and their prized possessions to the hop fields each day, and no doubt they were very similar to Wyclif's 'waynes'. These little carts had none of the coach built elegance of the aristocratic baby carriages, and when filled with several small children, were both heavy and unwieldy. Pictures of the period suggest that such methods of transport were only favoured by families who could afford nothing better, and the poor father is usually shown sweating profusely, as he pulls his burden along. They also make it clear that not only was it very hard work, but the man was a figure of derision—even to his own children. What was more, with his back to the cart and concentrating all his efforts on pulling the vehicle, he had little control over their behaviour, so that when they turned corners sharply, or went over rough ground, the cart was quite likely to topple over. Such labour was clearly not suitable for the lady of the family—who walked ahead in her Sunday best, carrying nothing heavier than a parasol!

Nevertheless, for want of a more efficient design, the baby carriage or wagon that could be pulled by a servant remained in vogue for over fifty years, and when Queen Victoria went for walks with her growing family at Windsor, she set the style of such outings. The Princess Royal with her brother, Edward, rode on their ponies—while a liveried footman pulled the toddler, Princess Alice, who was sitting up in her baby carriage, but the latest arrival, baby Alfred, was only entrusted to the safety of his nurse's arms.

When mothers and nurses had no strong man to help, they seem to have preferred to dispense with such awkward means of transport, and a park scene of the 1820s shows young children playing with their nannies, but there are no baby carriages in sight. At the end of the day, these nurses would have had to carry their tired charges home. No wonder that they were often loath to go on such walks, and liked to drag the older toddlers along by their leading strings, rather than carry them home in their arms.

However, during the 1840s there was a fundamental change in the design of these carriages that made them more convenient for mothers to manoeuvre. For instead of being pulled like a cart or wagon, they were now pushed from behind. Quite why it should have taken centuries to realise that it was easier to push such a vehicle, rather than to pull it, is a mystery. Baby transport seems to have been so bound up with the idea of a horse drawn carriage, that even when a man was substituted for the pony there was no reappraisal of the mechanics of the problem. The earliest examples of this new design were three-wheeled, and shaped rather like an invalid chair. They were intrinsically more stable, and considerably less effort was involved in making them move. So much so, that a painting of the royal family at Windsor shows the Queen's mother, the Duchess of Kent, pushing the heir to the throne in such a three-wheeler, without the aid of the customary manservant.

Almost overnight, these new carriages or perambulators, as they came to be called, appeared on the streets of London, and a Norfolk clergyman, the Reverend Benjamin Armstrong, was amazed to see so many on his visit to the metropolis in 1855 that he recorded this intriguing phenomenon in his diary.[11] Victorian ladies' magazines were quick to point out that no lady need feel ashamed to be seen pushing such a perambulator, whereas in pulling the previous chairs and baby carriages, she had been reduced to the level of a mere beast of burden! Royalty led the way, and when it was known that Queen Victoria had ordered no less than three of these new carriages, at four guineas each, their success was assured. Very soon the area around Oxford Street and Tottenham Court Road became the centre of the perambulator industry. They were beautifully made, often by coach builders, and ingenious variations in design allowed for more than one toddler to be carried at a time.

For these baby carriages, just like the ones they replaced, were only intended for older children to sit up in. Very small infants were still carried, as they had always been, in their nurses' arms. And it was not until the 1880s that prams were made that allowed the baby to lie down. Perhaps it was the improved springing and rubber wheels that persuaded parents to trust their tiny babies to such conveyances. Very soon the parks were filled with nannies pushing the latest addition to the family, in an elegant boat-shaped perambulator that was perched high above its tall wheels. Unfortunately, these were potentially unstable—and actually so—when the growing baby learnt how to bounce up and down in its well sprung carriage. And it was not uncommon for a child to fall out, when it was left unattended.

It was due to an increasing incidence of such accidents that the shallow pram fell into disfavour and was replaced by a much deeper model, which rested on small wheels, bringing its centre of gravity closer to the ground. Stability was thought to be of more importance than Edwardian elegance, and the introduction of factory-made pressed steel panels, that replaced the elaborate craftsmanship of the coach builders, meant that the price of such baby carriages came within the reach of most families. Such serviceable, if ugly, prams persisted until the 1930s, when concern was expressed that in the depths of their interiors the infant would lie in a pocket of stagnant air.[12] So the shallow-bodied perambulator became fashionable again, and was very similar in many ways to its Edwardian predecessor. And this design persisted until the '60s, when the advent of the family car brought about its final demise. For the new car-travelling family found the carrycot, with its detachable base that could be folded away in the boot of the car, or the baby buggy, much more adaptable to their way of life.

However, the arrival of a perambulator in the 1880s that was suitable for even newborn babies had one interesting consequence. The beautifully embroidered gowns that hung well below the baby's feet, and which had once so clearly defined the status and wealth of the child's family, could no longer be displayed in public. From this time onwards, babies' dresses became shorter, and the perambulator itself replaced them as the status symbol, with such names as Landau, Sandringham and Windsor. Nowadays a christening is the only time that the baby is ceremoniously carried in public—and the long and elaborate christening gown remains the only memorial to generations of nurses who carried babies everywhere in their arms.

9

The Christening

Nowadays it would be unusual to find a baby that had been taken to church for its christening before it was one week old, yet this was common practice in the past. Such urgency, of course, reflected the high level of infant mortality and it was taken for granted that many of these babies would not survive for long after birth. If their child died shortly after baptism, at least parents could console themselves with the thought that he was assured of a place in heaven, whereas if death supervened before the christening, there was no such consolation.

It was regarded as an unmitigated disaster for an infant to die unbaptised, and the sound of the wind wailing around the house on stormy nights was a constant reminder—if one were needed—of the importance of this sacrament. For such sounds were said to be the cries of the Gabble or Gabriel Hounds, the souls of unbaptised children who, robbed of their eternal inheritance, would hunt their despoiler, the Devil, for all eternity.[1] And to underline this loss, such babies were buried in the northernmost corner of the churchyard, in a patch of ground otherwise reserved for suicides.[2] But baptism was seen not only as a guarantee of spiritual happiness. In the days before any effective treatment was available for many of the common childhood illnesses, it was also regarded as the best form of protection against those capricious evil spirits that seemed on occasion to cause even the healthiest baby to sicken and die, while its parents looked helplessly on.

Few families were exempt from such tragedies and indeed until comparatively recent times, it was unusual for any parents to raise all their children to adult life. Most expected to suffer the loss of at least one child at some stage, and if it was only one, would count themselves lucky to have done rather better than most. As Dr Johnson wrote to Boswell on the death of his young son, 'you must remember that to keep three out of four is more than your share. Mrs Thrale has but four out of eleven.'³ Nor did the status and wealth of the family seem to afford any protection, and infant death was an unremarkable grief to parents of all classes. So much so, that even George III's son did not rate full court mourning when he died, because this Royal Prince was only a child.⁴

But although parents were accustomed to the grim facts of infant mortality, this did not stop them striving to prevent it in every way they knew. Worry about the baby's future health began even before its birth, and many a pregnant woman went in dread of seeing a hare, for fear that the split upper lip, that is characteristic of that animal, should be imprinted on her own unborn child. This belief that the sight of an object, particularly a frightening one, might transfer itself in some way to the developing infant, was widely held, and there was no limit to the number of things that were thought capable of causing such 'marks' as they were called. Older relatives and neighbours would give full rein to their imagination when it came to identifying the source of these birthmarks, and saw all sorts of signs in them, from a map of an island to the face of an animal. Although by the eighteenth century more rational thinkers, like Hugh Smith, were scornful of these old beliefs, it was agreed that they were unlikely to lose their appeal, since mothers always felt happier if they could attribute their child's disfigurement to some outside influence, rather than admit that the cause might lie within themselves. And to avoid any suspected malevolence even the hangings in the pregnant woman's bedroom were closely scrutinised. Should these reveal animals in their design, they were immediately taken down and replaced by others that contained nothing more threatening than flowers or plants.

There must have been quite a crowd in this room by the time the baby was born. For apart from the mother and midwife, and other female members of the family, there were also the prospective godparents, who had been summoned to the house as soon as the labour started. And in addition, by Elizabethan times, a family of any standing would also have had an astrologer to hand to cast the infant's horoscope for that moment when it gave its first cry. Such predictions were taken very seriously by parents, grateful for any help and guidance that might affect their baby's welfare. In fact, this forecast was so important that the astrologer was one of the only men, apart from the priest, who was permitted to enter the normally all-female preserve of the birthing chamber.

For less fortunate families who could not afford the services of such a gentleman, there were always folk rhymes which gave an intimation of the child's future, according to its day of birth, Wednesday, the day of woe, being the one that families would hope to avoid, while if they could manage the arrival on a Sunday they would feel assured of good health and happiness in abundance. But the puritans of New England were strangely at variance with this general approval of Sunday, and might even refuse baptism to a child born on this day. For they reasoned that the baby must also have been conceived on a Sunday, and to these religious extremists it seems no pleasure of any sort was allowed on the Sabbath![5]

Whatever the auguries, there was no doubt in anyone's mind that the time of greatest hazard for any baby was the few days between birth and baptism. Writers advised that the baby should never be left alone, for witches were said to kill a child while it slept, skilfully leaving no trace of their deed. Were these perhaps early examples of cot deaths? It was claimed that these wicked women were rejuvenated by the baby's blood, so to foil their intentions the cradle should be placed at the top of the house, as far away from the front door as possible. To get in, these evil spirits would first have to pass under the horseshoe that hung above the entrance porch, and the Devil was unlikely to try for he would be reminded that St Dunstan had once shod him with red hot shoes.[6] And to mislead any evil spirits still further, parents would never call their baby by its name until it had the protection of baptism.

It was even hoped that the furniture might help to safeguard the baby, and for this reason the cradle was usually made from ash or elder wood. The elder tree, reputed to have been used to make the Sacred Cross, was endowed as a result with a powerful protective influence, while the ash owed its reputation to a belief that was even older than Christianity, having been hallowed by the Druids.

Likewise, the piece of iron that was commonly placed near the infant, often as a needle threaded through its cap, owed its significance to a tradition that was pre-Christian in origin.[7] If the baby had to be left alone then the nurse would sprinkle salt around the cradle. For salt was thought to have the power to repel evil, and in Italy, when an abandoned infant was found with a small bag of salt round its neck, it was an indication to the rescuers that it had not yet had the protection of baptism.[8]

However, only the most desperate mother would allow her baby to be taken out of the house before it was christened, since outside the confines of the family home all manner of demons were thought to lie in wait for the tiny baby. One of the greatest fears in these first critical days of the baby's life was the possibility that the fairies would exchange the human child for one of their own. It was said that such fairy children could easily be recognised by their hard bloated stomachs, and their failure to thrive, even though they sucked their nurses dry. Presumably, many of these so called 'changelings' had some intestinal disorder, and the traditional remedy could not have improved their chances of survival. The idea was to torment the baby until the fairies took pity on its misery and claimed it back, replacing the human child in the process. In the Highlands, these infants were left on the shore at low tide and not rescued until the tide came in and they stopped crying![9] Such superstitions persisted, and as late as 1840 a man was sent for trial for abandoning his supposed changeling in a tree on Christmas Day. Pleading that his servants rather than himself were responsible, he was acquitted, although the subsequent fate of the child is not recorded.

Baptism was acknowledged to be a sovereign remedy against this wicked substitution in the cradle, but in the days before the child was christened, parents would be reassured if the baby had the protection of a caul. The delivery of the baby with its surrounding membranes still intact had been regarded as a singular piece of good fortune from ancient times, and the part of the membranes that covered the child's head was called the caul. Carefully dried, it was treasured by families as a sign of good luck and a powerful protection against evil. In the sixteenth century, Ambrose Paré was intrigued by the universality of this belief, and thought that it was probably due to the 'easy deliverance' which the intact membranes suggested.[10] But whatever the origins of this superstition, the caul was highly prized, not only as a protection against evil spirits, but also because it was widely held that the owner of such a talisman would never drown at sea. What is more, this protection could be transferred to subsequent owners, so that it was not unusual for them to be advertised for sale to 'naval gentlemen' in the eighteenth century, at twenty guineas apiece. This tradition seems to have been very strong amongst sailors, and C. J. S. Thompson records that they were still fetching anything between fifteen and thirty pounds in the London docks at the outbreak of the First World War, in 1914.[11]

But providing that the baby survived these first few critical days of life, and was apparently doing well, then arrangements would be made for the christening. Of course, if it should appear too ill even to survive the journey to the parish church, then baptism would take place at home. But in the normal course of events, the baby was carried to the church in the arms of its godmother, as the mother would be confined to her bed for another four weeks or more. The godmother would carry the swaddled baby, warmly wrapped in its bearing cloth or mantle, in procession with the child's father and other relatives. Even on this journey the baby was not reckoned to be entirely safe from evil spirits, and it was thought wise for the godmother to dispense some alms on behalf of the prospective Christian, and so some bread and cheese was usually given to the first poor person that the baby met on its way. Having reached the church porch, where the priest awaited them, the deed was as good as done, for even if the child died at this point, it was regarded as having received the sacrament by intention.

Greeting the christening party in the porch, the priest would first anoint the baby with oil and place some salt on its tongue. After this, the little group would move into the church and gather around the font. The baby was completely undressed, for total immersion was the rule in medieval times. But if it was thought that the child was too frail to be exposed to the cold, then it would remain clothed, and have no more than a token sprinkling of water on its head, and by the seventeenth century this modified ritual seems to have become the norm. During the exorcism which preceded the baptism, the north door of the church was left open for the Devil to make his escape, although no one was entirely happy that he had gone unless the child cried when the holy water was poured on its head. Indeed, if the baby did not cry during its baptism, it was thought likely to die within a few months.

After the baptism, the baby was anointed again, this time with the oil of chrism, and wrapped in a piece of linen. This chrisom cloth was a reminder of the white garment that was given to all prospective Christians in the early Church, and by the sixteenth century it was worn by the infant for the first month after its baptism. Should it die within this time, then it acted as a shroud, and such deaths were listed as Chrisoms in the Bills of Mortality.[12]

When Queen Elizabeth was baptised, her chrisom cloth was elabortely decorated with rubies and pearls. Three years later, her half brother Edward was born, and she was given the honour of carrying his chrisom cloth in the baptismal procession, although she was so small that she needed to be carried herself. This young prince, the only legitimate male heir to survive, in spite of all his father's endeavours for twenty-five years, was given a magnificent christening. Understandably though, Henry took no chances, and forbade the Marquess of Dorset to attend the ceremony, as he was thought to have recently stayed at Croydon where there was an outbreak of plague at that time. Even then, there were some three to four hundred guests, who trouped through the Queen's bedchamber three days after her delivery! She received them lying in bed, propped up on cushions, the room rehung for the occasion with new tapestries. The young prince was carried by Lady Exeter who, with the proud midwife in attendance, walked under a canopy. The King's eldest daughter, Mary, newly restored to her father's favour, acted as godmother and gave the baby Edward a gold cup as a christening gift.[13] But although the young Queen, with Henry beside her, appeared to enjoy the whole occasion, within twelve days she was dead, having succumbed to childbirth fever. Nor did her precious son survive to manhood, and by the time he was fifteen, he was also to die of a wasting illness that the doctors were helpless to prevent.

However, to return to the christening, it was customary to welcome the new Christian with a party, and there was considerable rejoicing that the most dangerous period of the child's life was now past. According to Aubrey, it was usual to give the father a special cake on these occasions, and caudle, a mixture of white wine, sugar and oatmeal, was liberally dispensed. Traditionally, the midwife went round the assembled guests with the baby in her arms, and received gifts from the gossips in return.[14] The wet nurse also seems to have received some sort of bonus from the family on this auspicious day, and when Mary Verney told her husband that the wet nurse's wages were high, she explained that this was because the nurse had not been paid the 'christening'. Her letters also expressed shock at the new puritan approach to baptism, with the godparents no longer in evidence and the father carrying the baby to church himself, without further ceremony. No wonder that she resolved to get a priest to the house to do it in the old way.[15]

By the eighteenth century, godparents seem to have been restored to favour. Usually there were three, with two of the same sex as the baby. And the baby wore a long gown rather than the traditional swaddling clothes. However, the gifts appear to have fallen in value, and a contemporary poem suggests that at times they were worth less than the hospitality that was offered in return by the family! In Norwich there is a small woven tray that was used for the collection of such presents, and if that were sufficient, then they must have been quite modest in size, if not value.

Just as today, things were given that would be of use to the small baby. Mugs, spoons and bowls were all traditional presents, and the gossips often gave a coral rattle to bring the child good luck. Items of clothing were also popular, but sometimes the gifts to a wealthy child must have been spectacular, like the miniature carriage given by the Duchess of Ormond to the infant Duke of Gloucester, Queen Anne's only surviving son.[16] Sadly, he was a sickly child, and at the age of eleven, in spite of all attempts to save him, he died, and with his death brought to an end all hope of succession for the House of Stuart.

But families did not need such examples to remind them that they must always be vigilant, and it is not surprising that even after baptism there was only a cautious optimism about the baby's future. For as Mrs Sharpe remarked, sometimes, in spite of all care and attention, the child grew thin and pined away. If witchcraft was the cause, then good prayers were the remedy. But this was not always the answer, in her opinion, and she was not beyond recommending corals and amulets as an extra source of protection for the baby.

It seems that there were more superstitions and customs associated with the first year of a child's life than with any other time. Naturally, some of these were concerned with the baby's future wealth and prosperity, and so, for instance, to attract riches the right hand should not be washed,[17] although for how long it would have been practical to observe this constraint, is not made clear. Likewise, when the baby left its mother's room for the first time, the nurse should carry him upstairs, to ensure that he would 'rise in the world' in later life. And if there was no upper storey then it was ingeniously suggested that the girl should stand on a chair, with the baby in her arms!

However, the great majority of such beliefs were directly concerned with the child's health, and it would have been a brave mother who ordered a mirror to be hung in the nursery. For according to superstition, if the infant glimpsed its own reflection before it was one year old—it was likely to be dogged by misfortune.[18] What parent would be game to test such a spine-chilling forecast? No wonder they were only too eager to trust any kind of talisman or ritual that promised to protect their helpless baby. Today, these customs and beliefs may appear to be quaint and rather naive, but they also reflect the grim reality of life for parents in former times. They in their turn, of course, would no doubt be horrified by present day Christians, who can afford to adopt a somewhat more leisurely approach to baptism, thanks to the dramatic improvement in infant mortality that has occurred in the last hundred years.

10

The Pot's Command

Considering the wealth of detail that surrounded other aspects of childcare, it seems strange that there should be so little information, before the nineteenth century, about the important subject of toilet training. Some historians of childhood have concluded that this was because early training was not attempted before that time. For they argue that if our ancestors were prepared to tolerate open drains running down the middle of their streets, they were hardly likely to have been upset by the problems of an untrained baby. But while it is true that there is little written instruction on the subject before the Victorian age, what evidence there is suggests that on the contrary, every effort was made to inculcate these habits as early as possible.

For dirt had been associated with disease from ancient times, and there was never any lack of advice about the importance of keeping the home clean and sweet smelling. And even though piped water was a rarity before the nineteenth century, this does not necessarily imply that houses were dirty before this period. In fact, paintings of domestic interiors often show a surprising degree of order, and children were invariably portrayed looking both neat and clean. While no doubt they wore their Sunday best for such paintings, they do suggest the prevailing standards of the time. But what is also clear is the enormous amount of effort that would have been necessary to maintain these standards in the absence of even a cold water supply. The endless washing and drying of nappies and swaddling clothes, especially in winter, and the lack of waterproof materials, would have made heavy demands on a mother's time. Under such circumstances, it seems far more

31 *Right:* A baby carriage that was built for the children of the 3rd Duke of Devonshire in 1730, designed to be pulled by a small pony.

32 *Below:* The three-wheeled perambulator of 1845.

33 *Opposite top:* The perambulator that was designed for a small baby to lie down in.

34 *Opposite bottom:* The more stable deep-bodied pram that was favoured until the 1930s when fears were expressed about the 'stagnant air' in its interior.

35 *Above:* A modern baby buggy that adapts to a newborn baby or toddler, and folds to fit inside a car when necessary.

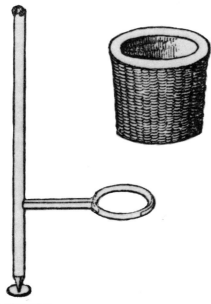

36 *Far left:* The Baby Walk or Gin.

37 *Left:* The Standing Stool.

38 *Below:* Child in Baby Chair. A bored toddler. Note the combined rattle and teething stick, and leading rein, which hang over the side of the chair.

39 'Woman making Lace' by Nicolaes Maes.
A Dutch interior of the 17th century. The baby is wearing a 'pudding'.
The closed front of his chair conceals a shelf below the seat for a
footstove, interchangeable with a potty when needed.

40 *Top:* 'The Christening' by Emma Brownlow.
The christening of recent admissions to the Foundling Hospital. Older children carry the babies to the font.

41 *Bottom:* 'The Christening Feast' by Jan Steen.
The celebration appears to be taking place in the mother's bedroom, with large quantities of egg-nog being liberally dispensed to the chattering guests.

42 'Foundling Girls in the Chapel' by Mrs S. Anderson.
An appealing picture of some of the foundlings.

43 Small children trying to learn their letters in a Dame School.

likely that, rather than delay, every effort would have been made to start this training as early as possible.

Just how this was achieved by earlier generations is not recorded, and it is not until the last century that we have any clear idea of the methods that were employed. At first sight this lack of instruction seems very curious, for although the Victorians may have been prudish in their reluctance to discuss such subjects openly, there is no evidence that their ancestors were so inhibited. But it seems likely that the details of this training were not noted because it was seen as no more than one aspect of woman's work that was so traditional that it did not merit further comment. For it had always been accepted that it was a woman's job to keep the swaddled baby clean and dry, and when he was released from his bands, the mother or nurse would have carried on with this chore. At the same time the subsequent toilet training, although tedious and time-consuming, was not likely to present any life-threatening problems to the infant, and as such, did not attract the attention of writers on children's matters.

But although little is known before the Victorian era of the methods of toilet training, it seems reasonable to assume that these were unchanged from previous centuries. For any radical change would have been more likely to provoke comment, and it is precisely this lack of comment which is so remarkable. Even so, Victorian advice, when it came, was often so veiled, presumably in view of the indelicacy of the whole subject, that one could be forgiven for overlooking it altogether. The 'good' child was said to be one who could not bear any dirt on his body or dress or in his surroundings for even the briefest time. And it was seen as the nanny's job to teach him both to love and achieve this cleanliness.[1] From contemporary accounts, it would seem that long spells on the pot were the usual method of attaining this goal, starting at the age of three months or even earlier in some cases. What evidence there is would suggest that this is also likely to have been the traditional approach to toilet training, for we know that Louis XIII spent many hours on his commode as a child,[2] and the design of potty chairs, with trays for toys and often a little heater in the base, would suggest that they were intended to be used for long periods at a time.

There the young baby would sit—miserable or amused—until

something happened. And sometimes it didn't! Then the experienced nanny would have recourse to a veritable armamentarium of purgatives—or even the dreaded soap stick. Certainly, his Royalty did not spare young Louis from the indignity of an enema on occasion. A woman doctor has recalled the terrors of such training in an Edwardian nursery, sitting with a sugar-topped biscuit on one side of her, as a reward, and a glass of castor oil on the other side should she be a 'bad' girl.

But by the 1920s, Pavlov's work on reflexes suggested that the whole question of training could be put on a more scientific basis, and indelicate or not, the *Mothercraft Manual* was prepared to commit the intimate details of such training to the printed page. According to the writer, the mother should make a practice of holding her baby over its potty just after a feed, from the very first week of life. For during these precious moments, it was very likely that a reflex bowel movement would occur. With repeated successes, the baby would eventually associate the cold metal rim of the potty on its bottom with this reflex, until finally it would only need this latter stimulus to trigger off a bowel action. One senses the writer's triumph in her claim that by such methods the baby would have no dirty nappies after the first few weeks of life, and very few wet ones.

Sadly, although the application of such techniques may have worked like a dream for Pavlov's dog, when it came to applying them to human babies they were by no means foolproof. For a start, they required a good deal of time and attention, and young mothers, without other domestic help, often found that this schedule dominated their entire day. Even nurseries that were well endowed with staff found such training methods demanding, for very young babies could not sit up without assistance, and the nurse was obliged to sit for long periods with the baby propped up on its potty, on her lap. A nurserymaid of the 1920s recalled the daily routine in after years. 'After breakfast, potting—What a performance! This was the high spot of our day, the most important event in it. Or events rather, because it happened incessantly. All through the morning, afternoon and evening, out came the pots. Out of nappies by ten months. It was the beginning, the very fundament of their training. Nowadays they don't start till two.'[3]

Waiting until the baby has reached two years old before embarking on toilet training has become the more acceptable method of the past thirty years or so. For with much earlier training there was often a problem when the child developed some voluntary control at about eighteen months of age. Under the iron discipline of the nanny-run nursery, this transition period may have gone smoothly, but young mothers were always writing to the problem page for advice about their previously trained infant, who suddenly became obstinate and refused to obey the pot's command. By the 1950s, the general availability of washing machines and disposable nappies had eased the laundry problem, and there was no longer any urgent need for early toilet training. A more relaxed approach was advised, and nowadays parents would prefer to wait until their child showed signs of being able to co-operate before embarking on such a programme.

But unfortunately for mothers in earlier centuries, there was no helpful reflex that could be manipulated to teach their baby bladder control in the first few months of its life. Parents would have to wait until the child was about eighteen months old before it was dry by both night and day. And some children would not achieve this control until they were much older. No doubt the long spells on the pot would have dealt with much of the problem by day, but bed-wetting always caused difficulties, particularly as the child grew older.

For while the baby continued to sleep in its cradle, the volume of laundry was limited. Dr Buchan had advised mothers to fill the child's mattress with bran, which was both cheap and easy to obtain, and could be changed as often as necessary.[4] However, bed-wetting was not nearly so easy to deal with as the child grew larger and graduated from its cradle to a bed. For there were no waterproof mattress covers available, and the bed was invariably shared with other members of the family. Under these circumstances, it is easy to appreciate the parents' concern when this aspect of toilet training was delayed. In 1472, Paolo Bagellardo had written of the sadness of parents 'when infants or boys beyond three years of age wet their beds regularly, not only every few days, but continually every night—and not only up to the age of five or six, but sometimes even into puberty'.[5]

Of course, the whole tiresome business of toilet training was not likely to have troubled those parents who sent their babies away to nurse, and may well have added to the attraction of such arrangements. For it would have been the nurse's job to teach her young charge these good habits, and her problem to deal with the dirty washing when the child was slow to learn, and most parents were probably blissfully ignorant of the methods that were employed. As we have seen, children that were sent away to nurse were usually returned to their own homes when they were about two years of age, and it is likely that most families would have delayed this homecoming until they were assured that this aspect of their child's education was complete.

But Paolo Bagellardo recognised that any emotional or physical upset might cause a regression of such recently acquired toilet training, and a previously dry child might return to bed-wetting if 'accidentally upset or disturbed by anger or unhappiness'. Such emotional disturbance was very likely for many children when they were removed from the nurse's care and returned to the alien environment of the parental home. No doubt quite a few of these toddlers, in spite of their nurses' assurances to their parents, would return to bed-wetting for a while, and it is significant that this is the aspect of toilet training that receives most attention from writers before the nineteenth century. Such families, nonplussed as to the reason for this behaviour, might blame the midwife for her carelessness at the time of the baby's birth. For it was generally held that if she accidentally allowed the umbilical stump to fall to the ground, the baby would become a confirmed bed-wetter,[6] and in some parts of the country the poor child would be fed 'mouse pie' as a remedy. James Primerose preferred that the mouse should be roasted,[7] but however it was prepared the prospect of having to eat such a delicacy the following morning must have concentrated the bed-wetter's mind quite wonderfully, and no doubt accounted for a good deal of its reputed success.

But there were as many causes put forward for bed-wetting as there were cures. None of which did much good. Probably the wise Mrs Sharpe got nearest to the cause when she suggested that the bladder-closing muscle was still weak, and Jacques Guillemeau gave the most helpful advice when he told parents to get their child up to spend a penny,[8] before they went to bed themselves. Fortunately, persistent bed-wetters are no longer subjected to mouse pie, but are more likely to find a cure with the help of the Buzzer. This ingenious invention only needs the first drop of urine to complete an electrical circuit, which in turn triggers off an alarm or buzzer. And the sleeping child is woken up before the rest of its bedding is soaked.

Clearly, it has never been easy to teach a small child clean habits, the more so when the baby was very young and unable to understand what was expected of him. But mothers and nurses were always anxious to start this training as early as possible, spurred on by the ever increasing load of dirty nappies and wet bed linen. Nowadays, when the washing machine has replaced the servant in most homes, there is no such urgency, and tales of rigorous toilet training régimes have hopefully been consigned to the annals of history. For, to mothers and advisors alike, the time and emotion involved no longer seem to be worth the effort.

11

When They Got Sick

Are the common children's illnesses of today—the measles, mumps and chicken pox—the same that worried parents in the past? Certainly, John of Gaddesden referred to 'mezils' in his writings in the fourteenth century,[1] but it is more difficult to be certain about some of the others. For until Pasteur's discovery that infectious illnesses were caused by specific micro-organisms, the recognition of an illness usually depended on finding a characteristic set of symptoms, and since many of these, such as fever and vomiting, were common to a variety of conditions, it was not always easy to distinguish between them.

Medieval references to childhood illnesses are understandably scanty, but it comes as a surprise to find a contemporary writer blaming overfeeding as a cause of premature death, a practice that is more often associated with the affluent consumer society of the twentieth century than that of the fourteenth. According to Berthold de Ratisbon, the offspring of a poor peasant was more likely to survive to manhood than the son of a knight, and he blamed this higher mortality on the noble ladies of the Household who would vie with one another to coax a little more pap into the cossetted infant.[2] But their anxiety to build up the baby's strength with plenty of food is understandable, for when an infectious illness struck a community it was the undernourished child who was most likely to perish. And a bad attack of measles was often so severe that it was confused with the dreaded smallpox.

When this frightening illness infected the young son of Edward II, John of Gaddesden was called to treat the royal patient.[3] His management was exemplary and he proudly recorded how he ordered the young prince's room to be hung with red cloth and his bed covered with blankets of the same colour to reduce the scarring caused by the pox. Whether the reflection of red from the spectrum did indeed prevent the disfiguring marks is difficult to say, but his treatment became standard practice, and Queen Elizabeth was nursed in this way when she contracted smallpox and very nearly died in the autumn of 1562.

No doubt the characteristic rashes of measles and smallpox were fairly easily recognised, but skin conditions seem to have been very common in the middle ages. This is not really surprising when one remembers that lice and fleas were the expected hazards in even the most respectable of homes. Their bites must have made children miserable, especially if they were tightly wrapped in swaddling clothes, and it is interesting that in an Elizabethan dialogue, the first question that the mother put to her child's nurse was whether or not the mark on the baby's thumb was a flea bite.[4]

At the same time the multitude of suggested cures for thrush over the years testifies to the lack of any really effective treatment for this condition. And mothers were always concerned when the tell-tale little white patches appeared on the inside of their baby's mouth, for they made feeding a sore and miserable process. Drawing three reeds through the infant's mouth before throwing them into the river was only one of the less practical suggestions for curing this common fungal infection,[5] and in many cases a more direct attack was made on the white patches by nurses armed with a piece of wool or rough linen.[6] But thrush was so common that many believed that you had to have it at least once in your lifetime, and if you were lucky enough to escape its miseries in childhood then it would surely catch up with you in old age on your deathbed.[7]

But this paucity of effective treatment did not dismay medieval parents for they firmly believed that God in his goodness had provided a cure in the plant kingdom for every condition that afflicted mankind. What was more, he had even given clues to the use of these herbal remedies, and so by the Doctrine of Signatures, as it was called, the yellow saffron plant should be used to treat bilious conditions while the long-necked Canterbury Bells were of help in throat infections. And when such remedies were given it was common to reinforce the placebo effect by making the child pray first that the medicine would do him good.[8]

But no treatment in the world seemed able to cope with the horrific effects of the Black Death which hit Europe in the years 1347–8. Even the healthiest individual, adult or child, could succumb, and often within a matter of hours. In many instances the victim was reported to have retired to bed apparently well, yet was dead by the following morning. Whether this epidemic was caused by the plague bacillus, or, as has more recently been suggested, by a virulent strain of anthrax, is debatable but the effects were catastrophic.[9] Whole communities were destroyed in a matter of weeks, in many cases leaving no one with the strength to bury the dead. A father in Siena recorded how he buried his five children with his own hands.[10] He seems to have been braver than most, for the corpses themselves were thought to be potent sources of infection, and a chronicler told of the appalling and unnatural sight of parents fleeing from their own sick children.

Certainly, physical contact with a plague victim or with a piece of his clothing was the likeliest method of catching the dreaded disease, but many believed that even a glance from the patient was sufficient to pass on the infection, and tried to protect their babies from this fatal 'fascination' or evil eye by hanging the phallic symbol of the Roman god, Fascinus, round their necks.[11]

Propitiation of pagan gods was only one of the many fanciful remedies against the Black Death, but on a more practical level it was recognised that if the victim could be isolated from the healthy community until he recovered, then the progress of the epidemic could be halted. And so, in walled cities, like the small republic of Ragusa, on the Adriatic coast of Italy, the City Fathers insisted that all newcomers should be isolated from the inhabitants for a period of forty days before they were regarded as free from infection.[12] This period of time, suggested by the length of Christ's wandering in the wilderness,[13] was to add a new word to our language, for the forty days or *quaranta giorni* as it was called became known to the rest of Europe as quarantine.

Similar reasoning lay behind Henry VIII's rules for the management of his precious son, Edward. For the death of his young wife, Jane Seymour, only two weeks after her delivery, more than ever emphasised the need for vigilance where infection was concerned, and the King himself drew up the régime for the Royal nursery.

The young prince's household was not to visit London in the summer, when the incidence of plague was at its height, and any sick person was immediately to be withdrawn from the nursery. High standards of cleanliness were maintained, and the prince's apartments were swept and scrubbed twice a day. All articles used by the prince were washed after use. But most important of all, no outsiders were to be admitted to the nursery without the King's express permission.[14] In this way it was hoped to bring up the young Edward in a state of healthy isolation.

But it was recognised that in some cases an illness would arise where there had been no evidence of any contact, however fleeting, with another victim. In such cases it was assumed that the infection had arisen spontaneously, by self generation from dirt and rotting vegetation. From such areas this unseen cloud, or miasma as it was called, would creep along the ground to envelop any victim who lay in its path. Rather like the recent Chernobyl disaster in Russia, this invisible threat caused panic, for there seemed to be no remedy apart from trying to avoid those areas where such a miasma might occur. It was for this reason that Dr Andrew Boorde, an Elizabethan physician, went into such detail when advising his readers where to build their home.[15] Marshy areas were to be avoided at all costs, and should his readers be unfortunate enough to live close to undrained land then he advised that all their windows should be firmly closed at nightfall to prevent the miasma seeping into their bedchamber while they slept. In fact this suggestion may well have protected them against malaria which was still endemic in this country, especially near marshy ground, until the seventeenth century. For the closed windows would have kept out any infected mosquitoes that were attracted to the lights of the house at night. However, if in spite of all these precautions the child did develop a fever then the windows would be completely sealed and a fire lit in the sick room to heat the patient. Hot drinks were also administered for the same reason. One can imagine just how disastrous such treatment would have been for the feverish child.

Dr Boorde's observations on the problem of late speaking children indicate an increasing awareness of the problems of infancy that was developing in the sixteenth century. Noting that all children however backward would make at least three sounds, he went on to attempt an interpretation. 'Acca' was an expression of joy or mirth. 'Aua' meant father—'Agon' a sound that indicated sorrow or pain. However he admitted defeat over 'wa' when babies cried, he had no idea what it could mean!

This developing interest in the needs of the young was also given by Thomas Phaire as his reason for writing the *Boke of Chyldren* for he aimed 'to do them good that have most need—that is to say children'. It was published in the 1540s, and he deliberately wrote in English rather than Latin to reach a wider audience. Like Dr Boorde, he believed that disease could occur by self generation, and that lice were exuded from the pores of the skin in this manner. He also listed the common conditions of children, and went on to suggest suitable remedies, noting at the same time that convulsions that were common in infancy did not necessarily develop into epilepsy in adult life. It is not surprising that such convulsions were common in Elizabethan children, for very high temperatures will often trigger off fits in small children, and as we have seen it was common practice to heat the fevered patient still further, while there were few remedies available to reduce the child's fever. Such seizures, once established in the course of an illness, could easily lead to death, and convulsions were a commonly recorded cause of infant mortality in the sixteenth and seventeenth centuries.

From this time onwards, these Bills of Mortality as they were called give valuable evidence of the common illnesses that affected Londoners, and children in particular. They were originally instituted in 1532 to give some advance warning to the Sovereign and his court of the approach of epidemics like the plague, but by the seventeenth century they were being kept on a regular basis throughout the year. Compiled from the evidence of two women searchers, who questioned the bereaved relatives, the diagnoses were often no more than the prevailing symptoms at the time of death but they do give an impression of the serious illnesses which afflicted young children at this time.

One of the most common causes of death amongst these young babies was 'summer diarrhoea'. Dr Walter Harris, writing in 1693, said that 'from the middle of July to the middle of September, these epidemic gripes of children are so common—that more infants affected with these do die in one month, than in the other three that are gentle'.[16] This diarrhoea probably arose from a number of immediate causes, but was basically due to a lack of hygiene in food preparation and storage, which was always at its worst in the hot summer months. Such epidemics were taken for granted, and they recurred each summer for centuries. And although they seem to have reached their zenith by the eighteenth century, as late as the summer of 1911 a staggering 32,000 babies under the age of one year died of this condition in Britain alone![17] But after the First World War, long before refrigerators were in general use, the incidence of this disease amongst children began to fall quite sharply. One theory as to the cause of this decline, after centuries of fatalities, was the disappearance of horse-drawn traffic with the arrival of the motor car. The resulting absence of horse droppings in the streets, which had always been a breeding ground for flies in summer, reduced the fly population in towns, and in consequence the diseases that were transmitted by them.

Naturally, the breast fed baby was safe from such infections, but any attempt to bring up small babies by hand in crowded and insanitary towns was always fraught with disaster, and probably accounted for the high infant mortality rate. On the whole, country children had a better chance of survival, although even these fortunates ran the risk of malaria if they lived in areas where mosquitoes were liable to breed. Although the connection with mosquitoes was unsuspected, the characteristic fever pattern of malaria was well recognised by Thomas Sydenham, and he achieved great success when he treated such fevers with quinine, a recent discovery from the New World. Because this eminent physician was a puritan, his religious views opposed the dissection of dead bodies and even the examination of tissues under the microscope, on the grounds that God would not wish for any unnatural probing into the details of his creation. He became instead an acute observer of the disease process and concluded that the fevered patient should be cooled rather than heated further. His patients were encouraged to remain out of bed for as long as possible and even at the height of a fever were only covered with a thin sheet or blanket.[18]

During the Commonwealth, he was a fashionable physician in London and in his writings referred for the first time to the 'hooping cough'. Other writers had described coughs but this was the first definite reference to whooping cough. It seems to have been very prevalent at that time, for in 1661 a mother wrote in a letter of the sad condition of her children who were troubled with the 'chin cofe' and she was afraid that it might kill them. There had been a virulent outbreak of this illness in her neighbourhood, and many children had perished. She described how as a precaution she left a light burning by her bedside all night so that she could go to them quickly when a paroxysm occurred, for at times they almost stopped breathing altogether. Fortunately, they were all to recover under her anxious care and the last we hear of them is when she requested her husband to bring home some sweets or lozenges for the young invalids.[19]

It was in the seventeenth century that rickets first made its appearance in the Bills of Mortality. Caused by malnutrition, its existence in previous centuries had probably been overshadowed by the more dramatic symptoms of scurvy, which, like rickets, was due to a vitamin deficiency. And although the underlying deficiency was unsuspected, successful treatments were sometimes chanced upon when remedies were tried that contained high levels of the necessary vitamins. Sir Thomas Browne wrote of rooks' livers being recommended in Norwich to cure childhood rickets,[20] and later in the eighteenth century the Manchester Royal Infirmary achieved success in this condition with cod liver oil, another rich source of Vitamin D.[21] Yet such treatments were largely unknown to parents in other parts of the kingdom, even though French and German doctors were sufficiently impressed by the Manchester régime to introduce similar ideas in their own countries. So even when a potential remedy was discovered, the knowledge of its success was not immediately available to all and the distribution of such medical information was patchy in the extreme. And as a consequence rickets, which may have been cured in Norfolk, was rampant in London while scurvy was often attributed in the puritan spirit of the times to a contagion that was spread by parents kissing their children.[22]

But the seventeenth century saw the end of the great epidemics of plague which had troubled the kingdom for centuries. After the great fire of London these outbreaks were a thing of the past, although why this should have been so is a mystery. Suggestions that the replacement of old wooden buildings by brick houses discouraged the breeding of vermin may have accounted for the City of London, but does not explain the disappearance of plague in the country as a whole. But whatever the cause, the feared epidemics did not recur although there were occasional contained outbreaks in different parts of the country: the last took place in Suffolk in the early years of this century, but by this time the disease had become much less virulent in character.[23]

Unfortunately smallpox did not disappear so easily, and in the seventeenth century this highly infectious viral illness was common amongst children. It was often lethal, and if the child recovered he was left with characteristic scarring of the face. But having survived an attack, however mild, the patient was then immune from further infection. So it was quite common for any employer to question a prospective servant about any childhood illness, and those who admitted to smallpox would be favoured for the post ahead of their rivals.[24] Mrs Boscawen found her whole family threatened by this disease when a footman, who had previously assured her of his immunity in this respect, developed the disease. Had this infection been confirmed, the whole household would have been quarantined together, and the illness spread to other members of the family. But the ever resourceful Mrs Boscawen wasted no time in smuggling him in a closed carriage to the home of an old woman who had had smallpox herself and could therefore nurse him in safety. Fourteen days later the footman died, but this quick thinking had prevented any further spread to the rest of the Boscawen household.[25]

However, in the middle east it had long been customary deliberately to provoke a mild attack of this disease in all young children by scratching fluid from a smallpox vesicle into the baby's skin. The resulting illness was usually mild, but conferred the same immunity on the child that a full blown attack would have done. Lady Mary Wortley Montagu, the wife of the English Ambassador to Turkey, was so impressed by this technique that she wrote home to a friend in 1717 that 'the smallpox—so fatal and so general amongst us, which is here entirely harmless by the invention of ingrafting which is the name they give it'.[26] She resolved to bring this useful invention to England and apothecaries soon became very experienced in such inoculations. She even persuaded the Princess of Wales to have the Royal children inoculated, but not before the method had been tried out first on six Newgate criminals, who were under sentence of death.[27] With the promise that they should go free if they recovered from the experiment, there seem to have been no further qualms about the morality of such an arrangement. Fortunately, the criminals escaped the death penalty, and got protection against the lethal smallpox into the bargain. The value of inoculation was soon appreciated, and the public-spirited Mrs Fry arranged for all the children in her neighbourhood to be protected without delay, while the Governors of the Foundling Hospital initiated a policy of inoculating all babies on admission to their institution.

After her earlier fright, Mrs Boscawan was quick to seize on this protection for her family and wrote to her husband, the Admiral, 'Pray Papa pray God to bless us for we are inoculated'. She then went on to describe how the apothecary had come to the house and without any fuss inoculated not only her four year old son, but his nursemaids as well.[28] While Dr Buchan, for his part, welcomed this wonderful protection against an often lethal disease and looked forward to the prospect of a similar protection against measles in the future.

It was later in the eighteenth century that Dr Jenner, a gloucestershire doctor, proved by a series of experiments that the milkmaids' belief that they could not catch smallpox, if they had already had cowpox, was true. Cowpox was a relatively mild illness and a deliberate infection with fluid from these vesicles, or vaccination, as it came to be called, was therefore intrinsically safer than the earlier practice of inoculation. For inoculation on occasions gave rise to a full blown case of smallpox, while at the worst vaccination would only produce an attack of cowpox, before immunity was attained. Inevitably, there were fears that vaccination would make the child look like a cow, but in spite of such doubts the value of vaccination was quickly recognised and the practice spread to the rest of Europe. Made compulsory in Bavaria in 1807 and in Denmark in 1810, it was not until 1853 that similar legislation was introduced into England.[29] This legal compulsion was rescinded in 1948, and in recent years this disease, a scourge of previous centuries, has been clinically eradicated and the need for vaccination—for so long a life-saving measure—has gone, it is hoped, for ever.

But there were no such prospects of protection against tuberculosis in the seventeenth and eighteenth centuries. Known by its older name of Consumption, it accounted for one-fifth of all deaths in the Bills of Mortality. It was a slow wasting disease that occasionally seemed capable of spontaneous remission. And it was probably a skin manifestation of this illness that was known as the King's Evil, which was thought to be cured by the Sovereign's blessing. Dr Johnson, as a small child, received such a laying on of hands from Queen Anne, the last monarch to follow this traditional practice. But tuberculosis was responsible for the deaths of many babies and young children, and in many cases the source of this infection was diseased cow's milk. However, once established in confined conditions, it was easily passed from one member of the family to another. Until 1882, when Robert Koch demonstrated the myobacteria tuberculosis under the microscope, there was no proof of its cause. Nor was any cure known, although sometimes the downhill course of the disease was halted by rest and good nourishment. It thrived in the overcrowded conditions of the expanding industrial towns of the nineteenth century, and amongst the poor it was a constant threat, particularly to the young child and growing adolescent. And because of its association with poverty, its occurrence in any family also had a rather shameful stigma.

In 1924, a vaccine was developed, the *Bacille Calmette Guérin*, or BCG, which gave protection to any child who might be exposed to the disease in future. At the present time this vaccine is offered to all adolescent children who are shown to have no naturally acquired immunity, and the incidence of infection in children has declined as a result. At the same time, during the past forty years specific drugs have been developed which are effective against the myobacteria should infection occur in spite of these precautions.

Even though tuberculosis was still a serious threat to young children in the eighteenth century, by the end of this period there was a slow but steady improvement in child mortality rates. No doubt inoculation, and later vaccination, contributed to these figures, but it seems likely that the major reason for this change was an overall improvement in the nation's diet, and because children are more vulnerable to the effects of malnutrition, to them in particular. And it was a growing awareness of the importance of infant health that led to the first hospital for poor children being founded in 1769.[30] Up to that time many hospitals had refused to admit children under two years of age, and even this hospital was only for out-patients. Founded by George Armstrong, the original premises were in Red Lion Square. It was open for four days a week, but few came on Saturdays as Dr Armstrong argued that poor parents would not—or could not— miss market day to bring their sick children to the hospital. It closed in 1781, and it was not until 1816 that another children's hospital was opened in London.[31] Perhaps this loss was more apparent than real, for the number of effective remedies available to treat serious illnesses was still very small, and the risk of cross infection would have been enormous, since it was common for patients to share beds, and no doubt diseases, in public institutions at that time. But as in previous centuries, there was no wonder cure available for most bacterial illnesses, and a child only survived if its natural defences were sufficient to overcome an infection. Many children must have succumbed to what would be regarded as a minor illness today.

The only light on the horizon for these children when they were very young was the invention of the incubator.[32] Dr Tarnier, an obstetrician and colleague of Professor Budin, was said to have been so concerned by the mortality rate in France after the Franco-Prussian war that he devised a special cradle for nursing sick and premature babies. He was inspired by the design of a warming chamber that was used to rear poultry, and in 1880 had a zoo keeper make a similar box for the Paris Maternité Hospital. It was called a *couveuse*, and a similar model was put on show at the Victorian Era Exhibition in Earl's Court in 1897, but medical opinion in this country was opposed to British babies being employed to demonstrate its use. Undaunted, Professor Budin arranged for suitable infants to be sent from Paris! Although the concept of the incubator was to make great advances in the care of premature babies, its origins owe more to the show ring than to the great academies of learning, for a year later a similar working model was on view at the Agricultural Hall in Islington. There the infants were on show to all who could afford the tuppence charged for admission while, we are told, on the opposite stand a cage of leopards was noted to emit an overwhelming odour.[32] Surely not ideal conditions for any baby—French or English.

During the nineteenth century the prospects for middle class children improved steadily, but amongst the poorer towns and industrial centres the picture was far grimmer. For until there was a safe supply of drinking water for all, cholera and typhoid took a tremendous toll on infant life. At the same time scarlet fever and diphtheria were diseases that spread fear in all parents' hearts, rich and poor alike. For when these diseases struck, there was little that they could do but watch by the bedside and pray that their child would survive. Nor were they always safe themselves, and Queen Victoria's daughter, Princess Alice, devotedly nursed her husband and children through an attack of diphtheria, but later succumbed herself after she had kissed her sick child on the forehead.[33]

Fortunately, by the 1890s it was discovered that the blood of convalescent diphtheria patients contained elements that would fight the disease in others, and the first use of this serum was dramatic. A scientist called Charles Sherrington had already developed the antitoxin, but although he had demonstrated its value in guinea pigs he had not yet used it on human beings, when he received a telegram to say that his own nephew was suffering from the illness. Met at the station by the family doctor, he was told, 'you can do what you like with the boy, he will not be alive by tea time'. He later described how he and the GP refilled small syringes time and time again to get the large volume of serum into the child. This task completed, the doctor left, clearly not expecting any immediate improvement. Yet by the early afternoon the child was already on the mend and after such success the antitoxin was soon developed commercially to prevent other children from dying from this dreadful disease.[34]

Although by 1923 a vaccine had been developed that would prevent children getting diphtheria in the first place, it was not widely taken up, and the incidence of diphtheria did not fall until a government backed vaccination campaign promoted its value during the Second World War. By the 1950s, small babies were also being protected against whooping cough by a vaccine that promised protection against this frightening infection. Sadly, the side effects of this vaccine in some cases were so disastrous that they brought the whole concept of immunisation into disrepute and there was a dramatic fall in the numbers of babies that were brought to vaccination clinics. Yet the incidence of poliomyelitis which rose to epidemic proportions after the Second World War was very successfully brought under control by the protection of the polio vaccine.

But even though the development of vaccines did much to improve the outlook for many children's illnesses, undoubtedly one of the greatest breakthroughs for children in the twentieth century has been the discovery of antibiotics. The development of the sulphonamide drugs, and later penicillin, led to the global distribution of these substances after the Second World War. The death of a small child in England today is not only a tragedy, but relatively rare, when compared with only seventy-seven years ago when 32,000 young babies died during the course of one summer from gastro-enteritis.

However, although antibiotics have had a most far reaching effect on children's health, it has been pointed out that it was haemophilia that was responsible for one of the greatest political changes this century. The uncontrollable bleeding which this illness can cause is inherited by male children from their mother. It had been recognised since Biblical times, and if there was evidence of this bleeding in the family, then a Jewish boy would not be circumcised in case he should bleed to death after the operation.

But in the last century, haemophilia became the Royal Disease when it afflicted the House of Windsor, and through marriage was passed on to many of the ruling families of Europe.[35] Queen Victoria seems to have been the first carrier of the illness in her family, and her youngest son Leopold, after many serious bleeds in childhood, finally died of a brain haemorrhage as a young man. Two of the Queen's daughters were also to inherit the trait from their mother, and through their dynastic marriages to pass the illness on to the Spanish Royal family and more importantly, in view of later political events, to the Romanovs who ruled Russia in the nineteenth century.

In 1904, after four daughters, the much longed for heir, Alexis, was born to the Tsar and his wife. It soon became clear that he was a further victim, when minor injuries provoked uncontrolled bleeding into his joints that often went on for days at a time. Even though by 1911 the inheritance pattern of this disease was becoming clear, there was still nothing that the doctors could do to cure it. So when it appeared that a strange Siberian miracle worker, Gregory Rasputin, was able to bring the crisis to an end by prayer, then his influence on the young Tsarevich's parents was profound. And it has been argued that by relying on this monk's judgement of political events, the Tsar ignored the counsel of more stable advisers and so made the Bolshevik revolution inevitable.

This tragic family was assassinated in 1918, but had the young Alexis survived he may well have benefited from the effects of blood transfusion, which was increasingly used from the 1920s onwards to cut short these bleeding attacks.[36] Later it became clear that the missing factor in haemophiliac blood, now called Factor VIII, was to be found in the plasma, and in the 1970s concentrates of this were given to haemophiliacs whenever they started to bleed. More recently Factor VIII has been developed synthetically by cloning techniques, and if all the trials in 1987 go according to plan it could mean that haemophiliacs no longer have to depend on blood products for their treatment.

But there are no precedents in history for organ transplants. When John Evelyn's talented five year old son died of liver disease in the seventeenth century, the possibility of replacing a diseased organ with a healthy one was beyond the wildest dreams of any parent. In recent years there have been enormous developments in this field and children have done particularly well since they appear to have less developed powers of rejection to the grafted organ. First kidney, and now liver, heart and lung transplants are all being carried out with great success in young children, who would otherwise have died. It was forecast by Ellen Kay that the twentieth century would be the century of the child,[37] and these advances in medicine, amongst many others in recent years, must surely have helped to make it so.

12

New Views For Old

Nowadays anyone who did not have a loving and secure childhood would rightly be regarded as deprived, yet this 'right to happiness' is a relatively new concept. Of course it is impossible to measure whether a modern child is more or less happy than his Elizabethan counterpart. For although potential causes of unhappiness like divorce were less of a threat to family life in the past, separation caused by death, particularly of the baby's mother in childbirth, was a very real hazard. And even though to modern eyes puritan family life seems harsh and even barbarous at times, such parents were probably not all that different from any others in trying to do the best that they could for their children. But attitudes to childhood have undergone enormous change over the years, and these are reflected in the way that children were brought up in the past.

Just how different these attitudes were is borne out by the legal status of the child in former centuries. The foundation stone for this thinking was the fourth commandment, which instructed the child to honour its father and mother. Unfortunately, this Biblical authority did not spell out any reciprocal obligation to the parents, so the baby had few rights in return, apart from the right to life itself. Generally he was regarded as the property of his parents, and they had complete freedom of judgement in his upbringing. This freedom was only likely to be questioned if the father was a vagrant or beggar. In such a case, the Elizabethan Poor Laws allowed the Parish to remove the child from his family and apprentice him to a master who would teach him a trade. But apart from this exception, the position of the parents, and the father in particular, was absolute. In fact, this 'ownership' was so strong that it was not until the Adoption Act of 1926 that it was possible to replace a child's natural parents.[1] Until this time, although others could act as guardians, the natural father still retained the right to reclaim his child, and his surname could not be changed.

In fact, the child had so little value in law, that it was not until 1814 that it became an offence to steal a baby from its parents, although curiously enough it was a crime to steal the clothes that he was wearing at the time of the kidnapping.[2] And by comparison with adult crimes, offences against infants were often treated with remarkable leniency. In 1761, for instance, at a time when a man might be hanged for stealing a loaf of bread, Anne Martin was sentenced to a mere two years' imprisonment for deliberately blinding children that she intended to use for begging.[3]

Unfortunately, this lack of legal standing did not protect children from the consequences of their own wrongdoing, and they were regarded as adults from the age of seven onwards. A girl of this age was hanged in Norwich, in the late eighteenth century, for stealing a petticoat. Sometimes such barbaric sentences were carried out on even younger children, and it is recorded that after the Gordon riots, a six year old was sentenced to death—pitifully crying for his mother as he reached the scaffold.[4]

Today, it seems unbelievable that civilised men and women should have turned out to watch such an execution. But although these were extreme examples, there were many who would have agreed that children were intrinsically inclined to wickedness, and needed very firm correction if they were not to go to hell. This idea that children were born with an inherent sinfulness had been around for a long time, and St Augustine had given it as his opinion that it was only the baby's weakness that prevented him from carrying through this wickedness.[5] Fortunately, most Christians believed that it only needed Baptism to put the whole business to rights, and set the infant on the path to heaven. So after receiving the sacrament, these little Christians could have all the cuddling that they liked, and the saintly Sir Thomas More reminded his own children in later life that he had always been ready to kiss them and only administered punishment with the weight of a peacock's feather.[6]

But the religious reformers of the sixteenth century questioned whether it was possible for a baby to be granted salvation so easily. Many thought that the child must positively choose the way of virtue and such a choice was not possible until it had reached the age of reason. Until that time, the baby was still to some extent under the influence of the Devil, and as James Janeway, the puritan preacher, reminded parents, they should always remember that 'their child was never too little to go to hell'.[7] Families who lived in this sort of religious atmosphere naturally interpreted a toddler's healthy naughtiness as evidence that the Devil was trying to claim their child for his own. And such behaviour was corrected with a harshness that often verged on cruelty. Roger Ascham related how Lady Jane Grey's life was made a misery by the tormenting of her parents, particularly her mother. She could do nothing right in their eyes and was always being punished for some supposed misdemeanour or other.[8]

Poor Charles Wesley was also brought up in this tradition, and we are told that the Wesley children were not only punished frequently for their wickedness, but even had to cry quietly, so as not to offend their elders still further![9] Such attitudes were deeply ingrained, and in his turn, Wesley criticised parents who allowed their children to waste their time in play. For he maintained that if they were permitted to do so when they were young, then they would find it a hard habit to break when they grew up. In fact, some moralists even condemned parents for enjoying the company of their children, for such an approach would only lead to indulgence, and that was not what parenthood was all about.

Fortunately, the fall of the Commonwealth and the Restoration of the Monarchy were to lead to a greater freedom in social manners, and this freedom was to extend to children as well. And although the puritanical approach was to persist in some families, for the majority there was a more indulgent attitude to childhood. This later developed, under the influence of writers such as Rousseau, into an acceptance of the essential goodness of the new born baby. A goodness, moreover, which these writers claimed was only too easily corrupted by the adult world. This was almost a complete reversal of earlier beliefs, and Wordsworth's image of the young baby being dragged away from the happiness of heaven at birth 'trailing clouds of glory' as he comes reflected this new feeling towards childhood.

Understandably, harsh punishments were no longer the order of the day, and a more relaxed approach was taken to discipline. Mrs Boscawen, faced with the prospect of correcting her son who had become rather spoilt following an illness, demonstrated this gentler touch. She wrote that 'the rod and I went down to breakfast with him', but the warning was enough, and it was not used.[10] All seem to have agreed that the poor were much less strict with their children, who were allowed a good deal of freedom. But no one could have been more indulged than the young Charles James Fox, whose father permitted him to ride into the dining room seated on a saddle of mutton, with his feet trailing in the gravy. Not to have allowed him to do so, in his father's opinion, would have broken his spirit and he reckoned that the world would do that soon enough anyway.[11]

But in spite of this newly discovered innocence, the young infant was still not shielded from the harsh realities of eighteenth-century life. It was quite common for children to be taken to public executions for 'their own good' and even tiny babies were expected to play their part in the elaborate rituals of mourning. When Queen Victoria's three year old daughter, Beatrice, wore black, following the death of a distant relative, her mother found nothing incongruous in the sight and commented on how charming she looked in her dismal clothes.[12] Yet in many respects Victoria and Albert were remarkably liberal in their attitude to their children's upbringing. We tend to think of them as stern and rigid parents, but they were both only twenty-one when their first child was born, and contrary to popular opinion, they actually approved of games and music in the nursery on Sundays, and often joined in these family entertainments.[13]

But Royal children had one great advantage over many of their subjects, for they never suffered the emotional upset that many children endured who were put out to nurse. In recent years a great emphasis has been placed on the early bonding between mother and child, a process that starts within hours of birth. When babies were sent to wet nurses, these emotional ties were made with the nurse, and broken abruptly two years or so later when the child was returned to its real parents. Many toddlers must have been bereft, and it is not surprising that there were problems of adjustment.

The Governors of the Foundling Hospital seem to have had some insight into the child's emotional turmoil. Perhaps this was because they had about ninety children returning from their nurses each year, and had plenty of experience. They allowed them to play for the first few days after their return, until they had had a chance to settle into their new surroundings. On one occasion a nurse so pined for the little girl who had been returned to the Hospital, that the child was sent back to her and they lived together 'happily everafter'.[14] But such fairy tale endings were exceptional. Fortunately, the practice of putting out to nurse seems to have gone out of fashion amongst well-to-do families in the early nineteenth century, but poor babies, especially if they were illegitimate, were still likely to be sent to the notorious baby farms until much later.

Today, the idea of sending a newborn baby away to another family for the first year or two of its life, seems extraordinary. For although parents would have avoided many of the worries of bringing up a small baby, they would also have been deprived of the happiness. And when, as frequently happened, the baby did not survive to return to its natural family, the period of mourning must often have been no more than a formality. And in this context, it is interesting that not only was it common to re-use a dead child's Christian name for a subsequent baby, but if a child seemed frail, and unlikely to survive, then a younger sibling might be given the same name, just in case the first should die! In such circumstances, it would seem likely that the dead child was soon replaced in its parents' emotions.[15]

Although this practice of sending babies away to wet nurses was common to many countries in Europe, the English always seem to have had a special reputation for coldness towards their children which puzzled foreigners. In the sixteenth century, an Italian diplomat in this country wrote of how 'the want of affection in the English is strongly manifested towards their children', and he went on to say that 'having kept them at home until they arrive at the age of seven or nine years at the utmost, they put them out both males and females to hard service in the houses of other people, binding them generally for another seven or nine years'. He added that 'few are born who are exempted'.[16] But although this idea seems to have been unique to England, he may have been mistaken in thinking that it showed a lack of parental concern, for it has been pointed out that this putting out was an accepted way of helping the child to make his way in the world. Introduced at an early age to a household of higher social standing than his own, he would be likely to find both employment and social advancement in later life. And it was this apprentice system that was used to deal with the growing problem of childhood poverty in the sixteenth century.

The grinding poverty that was experienced by many families in previous centuries must have had a great influence on parents' attitudes to their children. Today, we would have to look to a country of the third world to see the sort of conditions that many poor families suffered in the past. The poverty-stricken home, in which there was literally no food in the cupboard, no longer exists. When such parents were faced with the desperate fact of not knowing where their next meal was to come from, then their attitude to childhood was of necessity different from ours. Such children were seen as potential wage earners from a very early age. Samuel Crompton described how, when he had just learned to walk, his mother taught him to tread cotton in a barrel in order to clean it.[17] And Locke reckoned that children of three years of age were quite capable of earning their keep in the workhouse.

Not surprisingly, Dr Buchan and other medical writers deplored this early putting out to work, in conditions which often shortened a child's life. Nevertheless, child labour persisted through necessity, and women miners told Lord Shaftesbury's Commission that when they returned to the pit soon after child-birth, even their youngest children were a help in sharing the burden of pulling trucks along the mine shafts. The physical stunting which resulted from these practices was well recognised, and it was said of such paupers as late as 1870, that the boys were often too short to qualify for a career in the army, while the girls were excluded by their tiny stature from going into service with a 'good family'. Shaftesbury described these poor children on their way to the factory as looking like 'a mass of crooked alphabets'.[18] For such families, childhood would have been very short, and had little to do with happiness.

The State had been involved with the relief of such poverty since Elizabethan times, but the way in which this was done reflected the changing attitude to childhood. In the middle ages, as we have seen, the baby was regarded as the responsibility of his mother and father, and government only interfered when the family could not cope for one reason or another. The most common cause was the death of the parents, and in such cases wealthy orphans became Wards of the King. They were regarded as valuable pawns in the marriage market when they came of age, for the King had the right to bestow their hand in marriage on anyone he wished, while poor orphans had been cared for by various local charities on an ad hoc basis for centuries. Following the dissolution of the monasteries, some of these sources of organised charity were curtailed, which made the already increasing problems of vagrancy and poverty even more acute.

Government had been concerned about this problem for some time, and as early as 1524, the Spanish humanist, Ludovicus Vives, while living in England, had written a treatise on the best way to administer such poor relief.[19] He advocated a radical approach that he hoped would cure the problem for ever within one, or at the most two, generations. Rather than simply relieve the lot of the poor for the present, he argued that such people should be aided in every way to become self-supporting. Impoverished families should be given sufficient aid to bring up their children in comfort, and every attempt should be made to apprentice the children so that in later life they would no longer need to beg for a living. If necessary, the offspring of incorrigible vagrants should be taken away from them, to prevent them following their parents' lifestyle. By these methods, he hoped that the potential beggars and poor of the next generation would be eradicated. And simplistic though this theory may appear to us, with the advantage of hindsight, to the New Man of the Renaissance, it was a recipe for universal happiness.

An experiment run along these lines had been successful in Ypres, and William Marshall, a servant to Thomas Cromwell, wrote about it in 1535. And by 1552, the dissolved Priory of the Greyfriars in London was refounded as Christ's Hospital with the express purpose of aiding such poor children. It had places for 500 children, of which 100 young babies, or 'sucklings' were to be sent to nurses in the country until they were old enough to rejoin the Hospital. Although such an institution may seem small by modern standards, the actual numbers of poor children in need were not great. For instance, it was estimated that there were about 2,000 in need of relief in Norwich, the second largest city in the kingdom, with a population of about 15,000 people, and 1,000 of these paupers were children. So any attempt to relieve the problems of 500 small children in London would have had a considerable effect.

So confident were the city fathers of eradicating the problem of poverty within a few years by these means, that no expense was spared to make the venture a success. This money was initially provided on a voluntary basis by the City, but when this failed to meet the needs of the Hospital, rates were levied instead. Not only were the children exceptionally well fed, but they slept on feather beds—all the more remarkable as such mattresses were an unusual luxury for any child in the sixteenth century, let alone a poor one. Later, similar schemes were established in other towns, notably Norwich the largest industrial city outside London at that time. At the same time, the provision of outdoor relief seems to have been very generous. When a man with a large family found himself without a house to live in, he was granted twelve pence a week until such a time as the Parish could provide one for him. And written advice to overseers of Parish relief at the time counselled that 'those who God hath punished with poverty let no man seek to oppress with cruelty'.

Such schemes seem to have worked well although very soon the numbers of children that were eligible for admission to Christ's Hospital made the City specify that only legitimate children born in London itself should be accepted. During the course of the next century however, opinions were to change, partly due to the ever-increasing numbers of children, but also to the sad discovery as time went on, that with all the good will in the world, vagrancy and poverty could not be eradicated by these means. At the same time, the revenues that supported such foundations were failing, jeopardised by the effects of civil and foreign wars and finally by the disastrous Fire of London. Coincidentally, the puritan attitude to poverty was to favour harsher measures for dealing with such children. So by the seventeenth century, the earlier generous spirit which had lain behind attempts to relieve the lot of these poor children was all but extinguished. To the puritan, work was a virtue and poverty, if not exactly sinful, was not to be encouraged with sympathy and kindness. There was a sneaking feeling that if the poor were well fed, they would be not more, but less inclined to work, and idleness was most definitely a sin.

The need to supervise the pauper to prevent such idleness, and at the same time provide relief at the cheapest possible price, gave rise to the Workhouse. In such establishments, food and shelter would be given in return for work, which would help to offset the running costs of the institution. All able-bodied poor were expected to work, and three years of age was not considered too young to start. The earlier system of Elizabethan relief had not generally expected children to be put to work before the age of six or seven years. However, by the seventeenth century the climate of opinion had changed and it comes as a shock to read that Locke, normally regarded as a humanitarian, should have advocated that children of three years and upwards in these institutions should be fed bread, to which in winter a little warm water could be added.[20] Clearly, the age of Philanthropy was over.

Apart from the workhouses, aid continued to be given to families in want, but it was no longer given in the belief that the children should be brought up in security and comfort, but merely as the minimum necessary for subsistence. The Elizabethan Poor Laws had decreed that the poor were the responsibility of the Parish in which they were born. And no overseer would be popular if the rates he levied to pay for this relief were high, and so he was under pressure to keep the cost of such maintenance to the bare minimum. Abandoned babies, who became the responsibility of the Parish, were often put out to nurses for a fixed sum of money. The smaller the sum, the less likely was the baby to survive, but having discharged his legal duty, the overseer was not likely to have worried unduly about the high mortality rates amongst these unwanted babies. For their presence was a continual drain on the Parish, and when they died ratepayers were relieved of their support. Of course, this did not apply to every Parish, but by depending on such methods to relieve destitution, such an outcome was encouraged.

By the eighteenth century, the increase in numbers of poor and abandoned babies, and their early demise, became a national scandal. At the same time the effects of the industrial revolution were to exacerbate the problems of poor families and destitute children. Clearly, the relief given to such babies by the Parish, with all the inherent abuses of putting out to nurse, was no better than the workhouse, where young babies were cared for in the company of the old and sick. On the Continent, specialised institutions had long existed that cared only for children, and these had a good record. During James II's reign, there had been several attempts to found such children's homes in this country, but they made no headway, as it was generally believed that if such abandoned babies were too well cared for, it would appear that fecklessness and vice were rewarded, and the numbers would be encouraged to rise. But by the beginning of the eighteenth century, it was commonly feared that such continuing losses of young children would mean a future dearth of potential soldiers to defend the Kingdom. This seems to have been a persuasive argument, for in 1740 the long expected Foundling Hospital was opened.[21]

However unworthy some of the reasons for founding this institution may have been, it was to become an amazing social experiment. Initially it admitted about ninety babies a year, and these were very well cared for, and by the standards of the time, the mortality rates were exceptionally low. For about fifteen years, the Hospital was a model institution showing what could be done for the fortunate few who were admitted each year. Then, in 1756, when the Governors applied for a £10,000 grant from the Government, it was given on condition that they accepted all the babies that were offered—and Parliament would meet the extra costs that were involved. The result was a deluge, instead of about 100 babies a year, the numbers swelled at times to 100 infants each week. In all, over a four year period, 15,000 children were accepted, and Parliament was finally to pay £500,000. The powers-that-be were overwhelmed by the demand that this policy had unwittingly revealed. Clearly it could not go on, and it was brought to an end in 1760, when the Foundling Hospital once again reverted to its former policy of accepting about ninety babies each year.

Not unnaturally it was felt that a bottomless purse would be needed to fund such a scheme to care for destitute or abandoned children, and public opinion hardened. Some of the opprobrium for the failure fell on the Foundling Hospital itself, even though it had managed magnificently throughout, never ceasing, in spite of the numbers, to keep detailed accounts of its proceedings.

So this remarkable experiment by Parliament directly to aid all the destitute babies of London, had very quickly proved unmanageable, a result which Jonas Hanway, a governor of the Hospital, had foreseen with foreboding. After all, this four-year experiment had only applied to the infant poor of the capital; it would have had to be multiplied many times over to deal with the whole country's problems. Hanway advised that the Elizabethan Poor Laws, which were to remain unaltered until 1834, were still the best way of solving the problem of the destitute child, but that the manner in which the Parish administered that law should be carefully controlled in future. First, it was critical to know the extent of the problem. In the past many babies' lives had been so transient, that their very existence had not been acknowledged by the Parish. And Hanway's personal investigations into some of these London Parishes revealed that only a tiny minority of infants had survived.[22]

Public opinion was shocked by these revelations, and very soon a law was passed that compelled every London Parish to register all children under the age of four years that were receiving poor relief. It soon became clear that there was a wide divergence of care between one Parish and another, and the child mortality reflected this. To some extent, the more parsimonious overseers were shamed into improving their standards, while the better ones were encouraged to follow the Foundling Hospital's rules for the selection of wet nurses. Not only were these ladies carefully chosen, but if more than two babies died while in their care, then they ceased to be employed by the Parish. But good nurses were encouraged to look after their charges very carefully, for when the baby reached one year of age, or recovered from a serious illness, then they were rewarded for their skills with a small bonus, on top of their regular weekly payments. William Buchan was not alone in suggesting that similar premiums should be paid to all poor parents when their baby successfully completed its first year of life.[23] For he reasoned that if all parents were paid such a bonus, then poor families would see fertility as a blessing not a curse. But it was not until after the Second World War that the idea of such an allowance was to be become a reality in England.

Although some improvements did occur at Parish level as a result of Hanway's efforts, these results were largely confined to London. But for the rest of the country, the workhouse was to remain the mainstay of relief for destitute children. By the nineteenth century, most of these babies were illegitimate, since other charitable institutions always preferred to care for the 'respectable poor'. And after the amendment of the Poor Law in 1834, it was also extremely difficult for an unmarried mother to obtain outdoor relief for herself and her child. So it was the workhouse or nothing for most, especially as such a woman would have had great difficulty in finding work while she had her child with her. It is no wonder that many such mothers were driven to abandon their babies—or worse! As late as 1870, the bodies of 276 newborn babies were found in one year in the streets of London alone.[24]

There was a dramatic escalation in social problems of all kinds during the nineteenth century following the increase in population, which rose from nine million at the beginning of this period to a staggering twenty-six million at the end. But after the Government's unsuccessful experiment to deal with the problem of the destitute child in the previous century, even reformers like Lord Shaftesbury were reluctant to try again. And nothing which might be interpreted as undermining the rights and responsibilities of the parents was tolerated. For this reason compulsory education, which would delay the age at which a father could send his child to work, was disapproved of by Lord Shaftesbury, and did not become law in this country until 1880.

The introduction of other legislation to aid poor children was also slow, in some cases because parents saw the proposed reforms as imposing still further burdens on the family. As mentioned earlier, all attempts to register childminders, as a first step towards raising the standard of care, were strongly opposed by the poor, who knew that they would inevitably have to pay more for the privilege, and they had no money to spare. The more desperate were often relieved to pay for their child's care in a lump sum to the notorious proprietors of 'baby farms' just as the Parish overseer had done in preceding centuries, and with the same disastrous results. And it was not until a murder inquiry revealed evidence of what amounted to organised infanticide that anything was done about it.

In 1870, in the space of a few weeks, sixteen babies' bodies were found in the streets around Brixton and Peckham.[25] After further investigations, two sisters were arrested and sent for trial to the Old Bailey. It had been their practice to advertise in reputable newspapers, offering a good home and permanent adoption for a suitable baby. The unmarried mother who was looking for just such a solution for her unwanted baby, did not want any further publicity, and was no doubt grateful for the discretion and secrecy with which the whole transaction was handled. For a small cash sum, she would hand over her baby to one of the sisters, never to see him again. The two women would immediately pawn the baby clothes, and proceed to keep the baby asleep with laudanum until it died. Although the sums of money were small, trade was brisk, and they had ten 'sleeping' babies in the house in varying stages of neglect and malnutrition, when arrested. Sadly, only five of these infants were to recover after their rescue.

It was clear from the evidence at the trial that this was not an isolated case, and that there were many such establishments which reckoned so to neglect the unwanted children in their care, that their deaths were almost inevitable. Largely as a result of this case, legislation was introduced to register all such homes that cared for young children for more than twenty-four hours at a time, and should any of their charges die, then the death was to be reported to the coroner who would order an inquest unless a doctor had signed the death certificate. But although the public was horrified by the deliberate and callous murder of such babies, all attempts to widen the scope of the act to include shorter periods of childminding encountered such general opposition that they were dropped.

But cruelty and neglect was not confined to illegitimate children. The absolute right of the father over his family, which was enshrined in common law, was often responsible for a great deal of misery. And if a mother attempted to take her children away from a cruel husband, the law not only did not protect her, but would insist, if the father appealed, on the children being returned to his custody. In one instance, a baby of eight months was taken from its mother in spite of the fact that it was being breast fed. Even if the father died, the mother did not have the right to guardianship, and any guardian that the father appointed would have no obligation to consult her about the future welfare of her children. It was clear that the law needed to be changed, and in 1886 this absolute right of the father over his family was curtailed. After this date, a widow was entitled to have the custody of her children or to share the guardianship with another. More importantly, in any case of dispute between husband and wife, the courts were free for the first time to award custody to either parent 'having regard to the welfare of the child'.[26]

Of course the problems of child cruelty were not new, but many, like Lord Shaftesbury, felt that since much of it occurred within the family, it would be impossible to investigate without infringing the father's rights still further. There were great discussions as to whether a wife should be allowed to give such evidence against her husband, and whether the testimony of small children, who were too young to take the oath, could be admitted in law. Reformers in this country were impressed by the work of voluntary societies in the USA and decided in 1889 to band together the various voluntary agencies that were trying to alleviate child cruelty in this country, into a national society, the National Society for the Prevention of Cruelty to Children. And it was the NSPCC that was largely responsible for drafting the Prevention of Cruelty to Children Act, which became law that year and which allowed the authorities to remove a child that had been subject to wilful cruelty to a place of safety. Ironically, it was seventy-five years since a similar act had been passed to protect animals![27]

Over the following years, the NSPCC inspectors were called to investigate many cases of neglect and cruelty, but they could only proceed if this was shown to be wilful. Often the family situation was so bad that malnutrition and neglect were inevitable. Until the Compulsory Education Act of 1880, little had been known about the health of poor children in England. But the arrival of these urchins in the new elementary schools, often so hungry that they could not concentrate on their lessons, began to reveal for the first time the extent of the problem. And the end result of such childhood malnutrition was evident in 1901, when many recruits for the Boer War were found to be unfit for national service.

It was clear from all sides that if there was to be any improvement in the nation's health, it must begin with the children. And the legislation that was passed by Parliament from 1905 onwards, was to lay the foundations of the modern welfare state. This legislation provided that all births were notified to the local Medical Officer of Health, so that a health visitor could visit the family within the first week or so of the baby's birth, to give any assistance and advice that might be needed. And when the child reached school age, its health would be monitored by regular medical inspections in school, while the provision of free school dinners in elementary schools meant that needy children got at least one square meal a day. But this was not introduced without a struggle, for the extra expenditure meant that local authorities, in the absence of voluntary funds, had to charge an extra halfpenny on the rates. This provoked all the old arguments about how to aid the needy without at the same time encouraging the feckless poor.

Bad though these conditions were for poor families, the lot of the pauper child was worse. Investigations revealed that many such children were still brought up in the grim conditions of the local workhouse, even though all the evidence pointed to boarding out, or fostering, as the better solution from the child's point of view. A report from the Poor Law Commission at this time described the conditions in one such institution. The children were divided into rooms according to age and the toddlers had to sit at benches for their afternoon rest, leaning their heads forward on a long cushion to sleep. Meanwhile, in another room an older child sat with her feet in a bucket of water, as a cure for broken chilblains.[28]

The First World War increased the numbers of such children. Many were orphaned by the war, and still more were born to unmarried mothers who could not care for their babies. At the same time there was an increase in families who wished to adopt such children, often because they had lost sons of their own during the fighting. Many voluntary societies were set up to arrange such adoptions, but the majority of these agreements had no backing in law. The adopting parents could not get a birth certificate for their new baby in the family name, while at any time the natural mother could change her mind and ask for the child to be returned to her. Such insecurity was not only on the adopting parents' side, and if the baby did not measure up to their expectations, they were free, at any time, to return it to the institution from which it had come.

It was clear that the permanent adoption of a baby was likely to be its best chance of happiness, and so after much discussion, the Adoption Act of 1926 was passed. This provided legislation for a more permanent arrangement if parents wished. It allowed the child to have a birth certificate in the name of his adopting parents, and after adoption, the natural parents lost all rights to their child, and did not know the name of the new family. But the adopted baby still did not have the rights of inheritance that a natural child had from its parents and it was not until 1949 that this was changed.

Meanwhile, in the early 1930s the scope of the original provisions for protecting children from cruelty had been enlarged to take into custody children that were seen to be in need of care and protection. Although the laws that safeguarded such children had been extended enormously over the previous forty-five years, this legislation had been built up step by step, and as a result its administration was also piecemeal. No one authority was responsible for the welfare of children. Once more it was to be a horrific murder that drew public attention to the need for change in this direction. Three small brothers had been taken into care in 1939 because of parental neglect, and were boarded out to a succession of foster homes by the local authorities. In 1944, as a result of further systematic cruelty by the foster parents, the eldest child died, and this case became a national scandal.

Largely as a result of this case, a report was commissioned on the state of children in care, and it revealed that many cases were still being cared for in workhouse conditions. The Curtis Report, as this was known, described how such small children were still expected to have their afternoon rest sitting at long benches, with their heads resting on the desks in front of them. They also pointed out the pathetic attempts which smaller children made to attract the attention of any visitor, while the older children exhibited a dullness which they associated with the institutionalised child. They recommended that as many of these children as possible should either be fostered or adopted into families, to give them the chance of a normal upbringing. Most of these children were in care either because they were orphans or because their parents were unable to care for them for one reason or another. The report made it clear that these children had the right to security and happiness even though through no fault of their own they had been deprived of the means of achieving this.

It was the recommendations of the Curtis Report on the 'deprived child' that formed the basis of the 1948 Children's Act. And it was in this year that the Poor Law of 1834 was finally abolished.

A central authority was to be responsible for children's welfare. The Home Office was chosen, as the Ministries of Health and Education were thought to be too busy dealing with the new National Health Service and the provisions of the Education Act. This body was to authorise the setting up of Children's Committees in every Local Authority, and for the first time trained children's officers were to be employed to administer it. They would deal with all the problems of the deprived child. But it was not just the underprivileged that were to be helped by this postwar legislation. Indirectly, by means of free health care, child allowances, and schemes for national insurance and assistance, the State planned to aid all young parents to care for their children.

The setting up of this Department, and the increasing experience of the child care officers, soon showed that many of the problems of the young people that they dealt with could be traced back to the breakdown of the family. As a result, the Seebohm report in 1968 advised that children's problems should not be seen in isolation, but in terms of the whole family and community in which they lived. As a consequence the social services were grouped together under the aegis of the Department of Health and Social Security in 1970.[29] This emphasis on the importance of keeping the family together led to criticisms that in some cases the paramount importance of the child's welfare was not kept in mind. So in 1980, the Child Care Act re-emphasised the underlying principle to all such legislation, that decisions should always be made in the best interests of the child.

The structure of the family has changed considerably over the last hundred or so years, and it is unusual to find a family of six or seven children today, yet this was quite common in Victorian times. As a consequence, the relative smallness of the modern family has brought parents into much closer contact with every aspect of their children's lives. In addition, the length of time for which a parent is financially responsible for his offspring has been extended over this period. In 1880, elementary school children left school at ten years of age to earn their living and to contribute to the family income. Parents are still organising baby-sitters for children of this age today, and are expected to maintain them financially until they leave school at sixteen, or later, should they go on to further education.

In 1880, legislation was just being introduced to protect the deprived child. Today, a hundred years later, in spite of considerable legislation and an elaborate structure of social services to aid the child, it would seem that as one problem is solved, so another takes its place. And instead of solving the problem of child cruelty, we appear to be discovering more of it than ever before. Needless to say, financial resources are stretched to their maximum, and the need for more funding is a continual problem. Just as the Foundling Hospital discovered in the eighteenth century, it would seem that only a bottomless purse can satisfy all the demands.

But in looking back, it is also clear that the lot of children in general has improved enormously over this time, even though the hopes of the reformers may not have been completely fulfilled. When the City Fathers in Tudor times enacted their remarkable legislation for the care of destitute children, they did it in the belief that the problems of vagrancy would be solved within a generation. Such ideas were largely abandoned for more pragmatic solutions, when the Utopia they promised failed to materialise. And in the eighteenth century it was a fear that the nation would be left without strong fighting men in the future that finally persuaded public opinion of the need for a Foundling Hospital. Similar fears about the future health of the nation, and its effect on the economy, helped to silence opposition to the passage of welfare legislation in the early years of this century. But today the security of a loving home and good health is seen as every baby's birthright, and no further justification is needed for changes in legislation to help bring this about. Today, such legislation has only one aim, to do what is in the best interests of children, and so, hopefully, to bring them happiness.

Postscript

Christ's Hospital is now a co-educational boarding school situated near Horsham in Sussex. It still maintains its charitable status, charging fees according to the means of the child's family. However admission is no longer limited to residents of the City of London.

The Foundling Hospital was a well known feature of London until 1926, when it was decided to move the children to the healthier environs of the country, and eventually a new Foundling Hospital was built in Berkhampstead. By 1954 institutional care of this kind no longer seemed appropriate and the foundlings were transferred to individual foster homes. The Charity now concentrates on a Children's Centre for the under fives in the neighbourhood of Lambs Conduit Street, a special adoption and fostering project for children who for one reason or another are hard to place, and the provision of houses where adolescents without family support can turn for help.

Of the original buildings little remains, only the colonnades are still standing where Captain Coram would sit in his shabby red coat regaling the Foundlings with gingerbread. The site of the old Hospital is now a playground for children, and adults are only admitted if they are accompanied by a child. Somehow I think the spirit of Thomas Coram would approve.

References

1. HOW IT ALL BEGAN
1. *The Medieval Woman's Guide to Health*. Ed. Beryl Rowland. Croom Helm, 1981.
2. *Margaret Clitherow*. Mary Claridge. Burns Oates, 1966.
3. *Royal Confinements*. Jack Dewhurst. Weidenfeld & Nicolson, 1980.
4. *Mary Tudor*. H. F. M. Prescott. Eyre & Spottiswoode, 1940.
5. *Henrietta Maria*. Elizabeth Hamilton. Hamish Hamilton, 1976.
6. *Children's Costume in England*. P. Cunnington & A. Buck.
7. *The Happy Delivery of Women*. Jacques Guillemeau. 1612.
8. *The Midwives' Book*. Mrs Jane Sharpe. 1671.
9. *The Principles and Practice of Obstetrics*. J. B. DeLee. W. B. Saunders, 1940.
10. *Midwives and Medical Men*. Jean Donnison. Heinemann, 1977.
11. *Royal Confinements*. Jack Dewhurst.
12. *Victoria R. I.* Elizabeth Longford. Weidenfeld & Nicolson, 1964.
13. *The Story of Medicine*. Kenneth Walker. Hutchinson, 1954.
14. *The History of Paediatrics*. Sir George F. Still. Dawsons Pall Mall, 1965.
15. *The History of Childhood*. Ed. Lloyd de Mause. Souvenir Press.
16. *Virgins and Viragos*. Rosalind K. Marshall. Collins, 1983.
17. *Parents and Children in History*. David Hunt. Basic Books, 1970.
18. *Nursery Life 300 Years Ago*. Lucy Crump. Routledge, 1929.
19. *Royal Palaces*. Olwen Hedley. Robert Hale, 1972.
20. *Midwives and Medical Men*.
21. *Midwives and Medical Men*.
22. *The History of Childhood*.
23. *Book of Childcare*. Hugh Jolly. George Allen & Unwin, 1985.
24. *Advice to Mothers*. William Buchan. 1803.

2. BREAST IS BEST
1. *The Family, Sex and Marriage in England. 1500–1800*. Lawrence Stone. Weidenfeld & Nicolson, 1977.
2. *The Nursing of Children*. Jacques Guillemeau.
3. *The Boke of Chyldren*. Thomas Phaire. 1545.
4. *De Arte Medica Infantium*. Omnibonus Ferrarius. 1577.

5. *The History of Childhood Quarterly*. Vol. 4.
6. *The Midwives' Book*. Jane Sharpe. 1671.
7. *Elizabeth Fry*. Jane Whitney. Harrap, 1937.
8. *Letters to Married Woman on the Nursing and Management of Children*. Hugh Smith.
9. *Advice to Mothers*. William Buchan. 1803.
10. *A History of Infant Feeding*. Ian G. Wickes. 1953.
11. *The Story of the Nursery*. Magdalen King-Hall. Routledge & Kegan Paul, 1958.
12. *Parents and Children in History*. David Hunt. Basic Books, 1970.
13. *The Rise and Fall of the British Nanny*. J. Gathorne-Hardy. Hodder and Stoughton, 1972.
14. *The History of Childhood*.
15. *The Father of Child Care*. Life of William Cadogan. M. & J. Rendle Short. J. Wright & Sons Ltd. Bristol, 1966.
16. *The Countess of Lincolnes Nurserie* by Elizabeth Clinton. Dowager Countess of Lincoln. Oxford, 1622.
17. *The Family, Sex and Marriage*.
18. *A History of Infant Feeding*. Wickes.
19. *The Story of the Nursery*.
20. *Victoria R. I.* Elizabeth Longford. Weidenfeld & Nicolson, 1964.
21. & 22. *Victoria and her Daughters*. Nina Epton. Weidenfeld & Nicolson, 1971.

3. BORROWED MILK

1. *Medieval Lore*. Robert Steele. 1905.
2. *The Myth of Motherhood*. Elizabeth Badinter. Souvenir Press, 1981.
3. *The History of Childhood*. Ed. Lloyd de Mause. Souvenir Press.
4. *The Myth of Motherhood*.
5. *The History of Childhood*.
6. *The Englishman's Food*. J. C. Drummond & A. Wilbraham. Jonathan Cape, 1958.
7. *The History of Paediatrics*. G. F. Still. Dawsons, 1965.
8. *The Rise and Fall of the British Nanny*. J. Gathorne-Hardy. 1972.
9. *Lives of the Artists*. Giorgio Vasari. Penguin Books.
10. *The History of Infant Feeding from Elizabethan Times*. David Forsyth.
11. *Medieval Panorama*. G. G. Coulton. C. U. P., 1938.
12. *The Nursing of Children*. Jacques Guillemeau. 1612.
13. *The Victorian Family*. Ed. Anthony S. Wohl. Croom Helm, 1978.
14. *The Nursing of Children*.
15. *Memoirs of the Verney Family*. Ed. Frances & Mary Verney. 1925.
16. *Queen Anne's Son*. Hester W. Chapman. Andre Deutsch, 1954.
17. *The Story of the Nursery*. Magdalen King-Hall. Routledge & Kegan Paul.
18. *The History of Childhood*.
19. *Edward VI, The Young King*. W. K. Jordan. George Allen & Unwin Ltd.
20. & 21. *The History of Paediatrics*.
22. *Diseases of Infants*. Walter Harris. 1693.
23. *The History of Childhood*.

24. *The Myth of Motherhood.*
25. *The Nursling.* Pierre Budin. 1907.
26. *The Diary of Benjamin Robert Haydon.* Ed. Williard Bissell-Pope. Harvard University Press, 1963.

4. HOW SHALL WE FEED THE BABY?
1. *A History of Infant Feeding.* Ian G. Wickes. 1952.
2. *Nursing Mirror.* 30.11.1983. Midwifery Forum 10. Rosalind Marshall.
3. *Queen Over The Water.* Mary Hopkirk. John Murray, 1953.
4. *The History of Infant Feeding from Elizabethan Times.* David Forsyth MD.
5. *Infant Feeding by Artificial Means.* S. H. Sadler.
6. *Housekeeping in the 18th Century.* Rosamond Bayne-Powell. 1956.
7. *The Englishman's Food.* J. C. Drummond & A. Wilbraham. Jonathan Cape, 1958.
8. *The History of Infant Feeding from Elizabethan Times.*
9. *The Englishman's Food.*
10. *A History of Infant Feeding.*
11. *A History of Infant Feeding.*
12. *Infantilia, the Archeology of the Nursery.* A. Dobson & M. Lewis. 1971.
13. *The History of Infant Feeding from Elizabethan Times.* David Forsyth.
14. *The Englishman's Food.*
15. *Ten Years of Infant Feeding 1974–1984.* Cow & Gate.
16. *The Englishman's Food.*
17. *The Nursling.* Pierre Budin.
18. *Children in English Society.*
19. *The History of Paediatrics.* G. F. Still.

5. WEANING AND THE PERILS OF TEETHING
1. *Royal Children.* Dulcie M. Ashdown. Robert Hale, 1979.
2. *A History of Infant Feeding.* David Forsyth. 1910.
3. *The History of Childhood.*
4. *Medieval Lore.*
5. *Parents and Children in History.* David Hunt. 1970.
6. *Nursery Life 300 Years Ago.* Lucy Crump. Geo. Routledge & Sons Ltd, 1929.
7. *Parents and Children in History.*
8. *A General Treatise on the Diseases of Infants and Children.* John Pechy. 1697.
9. *The English Child in the 18th Century.* R. Bayne-Powell. John Murray, 1939.
10. *English Home Life.* Christina Hole. Batsford, 1947.
11. *Parents and Children in History.*
12. *History of Paediatrics.*
13. *History of Paediatrics.*
14. *The Years of the Nannies.* Mary Ann Gibbs. Hutchinson, 1960.
15. *Parents and Children in History.*
16. *The Englishman's Food.*
17. *Children in English Society.*
18. *The Englishman's Food.*

6. ALL WRAPPED UP

1. *The English Child in the 18th Century*. R. Bayne-Powell. 1939. and *Children's Costume in England*.
2. *The Midwives' Book*. Mrs Jane Sharpe.
3. *The History of Childhood*.
4. *The Story of the Nursery*.
5. *The Story of the Nursery*.
6. The wax effigy of the Spanish or Portuguese infant Don Santiago de la Haza y Laguna is to be found in the Bethnal Green Museum of Childhood.
7. *Children's Costume in England*. P. Cunnington & C. Lucas. A. & C. Black, 1965.
8. *A General Treatise of the Diseases of Infants and Children*. John Pechey. 1697.
9. *Costumes for Births, Marriages and Deaths*. P. Cunnington & C. Lucas.
10. *The History of Childhood*.
11. *Lives of the Princesses of England*. Mary Ann Everett-Green. 1881.
12. *Children's Costume in England*.
13. *History of Children's Costume*. Elizabeth Ewing. Bibliophile, 1977.
14. *History of Children's Costume*.
15. *Queen Victoria's Children*.
16. *History of Children's Costume*.
17. *The Mechanical Baby*.
18. *Some Thoughts Concerning Education*. John Locke.

7. MINDING THE BABY

1. *Homes of Other Days*. Thomas Wright. Trubner & Co, 1871.
2. *De Arte Medica Infantum*. Omnibonus Ferrarius. 1577. *History of Paediatrics*.
3. *A Regimen for Young Children*. Batholomew Metlinger. 1473. *The Mechanical Baby*. Daniel Beekman. Dobson Books, 1977.
4. *The Children's Book*. Felix Wurtz. 1563. *The History of Childhood*.
5. *Childhood in 17th Century Scotland*. Rosalind K. Marshall. 1976.
6. *Childhood in 17th Century Scotland*.
7. *Nollekens and His Times*. John Thomas Smith.
8. *Nollekens and His Times*.
9. *Nollekens and His Times*.
10. *Memoirs of the Verney Family*. Ed. Frances & Mary Verney. Longmans, 1925.
11. *The English Child in the 18th Century*. R. Bayne-Powell. 1939.
12. *The Voices of Children*. Irina Strickland. Basil Blackwell, 1973.
13. *Children in English Society*. Ivy Pinchbeck & Margaret Hewitt. 1969.
14. *Children in English Society*.
15. *Children in English Society*.
16. *History of the Foundling Hospital*. R. H. Nichols. & F. A. Wray. O.U.P., 1935.
17. *Jonas Hanway*. John H. Hutchins. 1940.
18. *Children in English Society*.

19. *Jonas Hanway*.
20. *Barnardo*. Gillian Wagner. Weidenfeld & Nicolson, 1979.

8. MOVING AROUND

1. *The Story of the Nursery*. Magdalen King-Hall. Routledge & Kegan Paul, 1958.
2. *The History of Childhood*. Ed. Lloyd de Mause. Souvenir Press.
3. *Edward VI, The Young King*. W. K. Jordan. George Allen & Unwin.
4. *The Mechanical Baby*. Daniel Beekman. Dobson Books, 1979.
5. *The History of Childhood*.
6. *The Queen's Wards*. J. Hurstfield. 1958.
7. *Memoirs of the Verney Family*.
8. *Lives of the Princesses of England*. Mary Anne Everatt Green. 1851.
9. *The Admiral's Wife*. Cecil Aspinell-Oglander. Longmans.
10. *Queen Anne's Son*. Hester W. Chapman. Andre Deutsch, 1954.
11. *Prams, Mailcarts and Bassinets*. Jack Hampshire.
12. *The Mothercraft Manual*. Mabel Liddiard. J. & A. Churchill Ltd, 1923.

9. THE CHRISTENING

1. *The Story of the Nursery*.
2. *English Home Life*. Christina Hole. Batsford, 1947.
3. *Housekeeping in the 18th Century*. Rosamond Bayne-Powell.
4. *The Years of the Nannies*. Mary Ann Gibbs. Hutchinson, 1960.
5. *Sex in History*. Reay Tannahill. Hamish Hamilton, 1980.
6. *The English Child in the 18th Century*.
7. *The English Child in the 18th Century*.
8. *The History of Childhood Quarterly*. Vol. 1. No. 2. 'The Foundlings of Florence'.
9. *The Hand of Destiny*. C. J. S. Thompson. Rider & Co, 1932.
10. *The Hand of Destiny*.
11. *The Hand of Destiny*.
12. *Costumes for Birth, Marriages and Death*. P. Cunnington & C. Lucas, 1972.
13. *The Last Tudor King*. Hester W. Chapman. Jonathan Cape, 1958.
14. *Midwives and Medical Men*. Jean Donnison. Heinemann, 1977.
15. *Memoirs of the Verney Family*.
16. *Queen Anne's Son*. Hester W. Chapman. Andre Deutsch, 1954.
17. *The English Child in the 18th Century*.
18. *The Hand of Destiny*.

10. THE POT'S COMMAND

1. *The Rise and Fall of the British Nanny*. J. Gathorne-Hardy. Hodder & Stoughton, 1972.
2. *The History of Childhood*.
3. *The Rise and Fall of the British Nanny*.

4. *Advice to Mothers*. William Buchan MD. 1803.
5. *The Mechanical Baby*.
6. *Pediatrics*. American Academy of Pediatrics. August 1977.
7. *The History of Paediatrics*.
8. *The Nursing of Children*. Jacques Guillemeau. 1612.

11. WHEN THEY GOT SICK

1. *Epidemic Diseases*. A. H. Gale. Pelican Books, 1959.
2. *A Medieval Garner*. G. G. Coulton. 1910.
3. *The Hand of Destiny*. C. J. S. Thompson. Rider & Co, 1932.
4. *The Elizabethan Home*. M. St Clare Byrne. Methuen & Co Ltd, 1949.
5. *Housekeeping in the 18th Century*. R. Bayne-Powell.
6. *The Mechanical Baby*. Daniel Beekman.
7. *The English Child in the 18th Century*. R. Bayne-Powell.
8. *The Hand of Destiny*.
9. *The Black Death*. Graham Twigg. Batsford, 1984.
10. *The Black Death*. Philip Ziegler. Collins, 1969.
11. *The Hand of Destiny*.
12. *The Story of Medicine*. Kenneth Walker. Arrow Books, 1959.
13. *The Black Death*. Philip Ziegler.
14. *The Last Tudor King*. Hester W. Chapman. Jonathan Cape, 1958.
15. *The First Book of the Introduction to Knowledge*. Andrew Boorde.
16. *Diseases of Infants*. Dr Walter Harris. 1693.
17. *Epidemic Diseases*. A. H. Gale. Pelican Books.
18. *Dr Thomas Sydenham*. Kenneth Dewhurst. Wellcome Historical Library.
19. *Epidemic Diseases*.
20. *The Englishman's Food*.
21. *The Englishman's Food*.
22. *The Englishman's Food*.
23. *Epidemic Diseases*.
24. *English Home Life*. Christina Hole. Batsford Books, 1947.
25. *The Admiral's Wife*. Cecil Aspinall-Oglander. Longmans, 1940.
26. *The History of Paediatrics*.
27. *The Father of Child Care*. M. & J. Rendle-Short. J. Wright & Sons, 1966.
28. *The Admiral's Wife*.
29. *Epidemic Diseases*.
30. *The History of Paediatrics*.
31. *A History of Infant Feeding*. Ian G. Wickes.
32. William A. Silverman MD. Pediatrics. Vol 64. Aug 1979. No 2. American Academy of Pediatrics.
33. *Victoria and her Daughters*. Nina Epton. 1971.
34. *Cabbages and Kings*. Grant Uden & Roy Yglesias. Kestrel Books, 1978.
35. *Nicholas and Alexandra*. Robert K. Massie. World Books, 1969.
36. *The History of Haemophilia*. G. I. C. Ingram. 1975.
37. *The History of Childhood*.

12. NEW VIEWS FOR OLD

1. *Children in English Society.* Ivy Pinchbeck & Margaret Hewitt. 1969.
2. *Children in English Society.*
3. *Children in English Society.*
4. *The English Child in the 18th Century.* R. Bayne-Powell.
5. *The Myth of Motherhood.* Elizabeth Badinter. Souvenir Press, 1981.
6. *The Family, Sex and Marriage.* Lawrence Stone.
7. *The Story of the Nursery.* Magdalen King-Hall.
8. *Children in English Society.*
9. *The Family, Sex and Marriage.*
10. *The Admiral's Wife.*
11. *Children in English Society.*
12. *Mourning Dress.* Lou Taylor. George Allen & Unwin, 1983.
13. *Queen Victoria's Children.* Daphne Bennett. Victor Gollancz, 1980.
14. *The History of the Foundling Hospital.* R. H. Nichols & F. A. Wray. O.U.P., 1935.
15. *The Family, Sex and Marriage.*
16. *The Rise and Fall of the British Nanny.*
17. *Children in English Society.*
18. *Children in English Society.*
19. *Children in English Society.*
20. *Some Thoughts Concerning Education.*
21. *The History of the Foundling Hospital.*
22. *Children in English Society.*
23. *Advice to Mothers.* William Buchan. 1803.
24. 25. 26. 27. & 28. *Children in English Society.*
29. *Introduction to the Social Services.* W. E. Bough. Macmillan, 1983.